Relating to

as Jesus Would

A Guided Discovery for Groups and Individuals
Kevin Perrotta

LOYOLAPRESS.
CHICAGO

LOYOLAPRESS.

3441 N. ASHLAND AVENUE
CHICAGO, ILLINOIS 60657
(800) 621-1008
WWW.LOYOLAPRESS.ORG

Nihil Obstat
Reverend John G. Lodge, S.S.L., S.T.D.
Censor Deputatus
June 25, 2004

Imprimatur
Most Reverend Edwin M. Conway, D.D.
Vicar General
Archdiocese of Chicago
June 29, 2004

The *Nihil Obstat* and *Imprimatur* are official declarations that a book is free of doctrinal and moral error. No implication is contained therein that those who have granted the *Nihil Obstat* and *Imprimatur* agree with the content, opinions, or statements expressed.

The Scripture quotations contained herein are from the New Revised Standard Version Bible: Catholic Edition, copyright © 1993 and 1989 by the Division of Christian Education of the National Council of the Churches of Christ in the U.S.A. Used by permission. All rights reserved. Subheadings in Scripture quotations have been added by the author.

The quotation from Giacomo Benincasa (p. 23) is taken from Igino Giordani, *Catherine of Siena: Fire and Blood,* trans. Thomas J. Tobin, (Milwaukee, Wisc.: Bruce Pub. Co., 1959).

The Latin text of St. Augustine's commentary on John 8 (p. 47) can be found in J. P. Migne, *Patrologia Latina* (Paris, 1864), vol. 35. The translation is by Kevin Perrotta. An English translation of the entire commentary is available in the Fathers of the Church series, translated by John W. Rettig (Washington, D.C.: Catholic University of America Press), four volumes.

"Bethany Decisions," by Irene Zimmerman, O.S.F. (p. 83) Copyright 2004, Irene Zimmerman. All rights reserved. Poem is reprinted from *Incarnation: New and Selected Poems for Spiritual Reflection* by Irene Zimmerman; published by Cowley Publications, 4 Brattle St., Cambridge, MA 02138. www.cowley.org (800-225-1534).

Interior design by Kay Hartmann/Communique Design
Illustration by Anni Betts

ISBN 0-8294-2065-7

Printed in the United States of America
05 06 07 08 09 10 Bang 10 9 8 7 6 5 4 3 2 1

Contents

4 *How to Use This Guide*

6 *The Importance of Asking the Right Question*

12 **Week 1**
Jesus' Way of Relating to His Family
Selections from Luke 2; John 2; 7; Mark 3

24 **Week 2**
. . . to Seekers
Selections from John 2–3; Luke 7;
Mark 10; 12

36 **Week 3**
. . . to Those Known as Sinners
Selections from Luke 5; 7; John 8; Luke 23

48 **Week 4**
. . . to People He Met along the Way
Selections from Luke 12; Mark 10;
Luke 19; 23

60 **Week 5**
. . . to Those Who Rejected Him
Selections from Luke 9; 11; Mark 11;
John 18–19; Luke 23

72 **Week 6**
. . . to His Friends
Selections from Luke 10; John 11;12

84 *A Closer Look at Jesus' Family*

90 *Suggestions for Bible Discussion Groups*

93 *Suggestions for Individuals*

94 *Resources*

How to Use This Guide

If you want to know about Jesus, the natural place to begin is the Gospels. In the Gospels we can discover Jesus for the first time—or rediscover him for the thousandth time.

In this book we will read some excerpts from the Gospels in order to examine how Jesus related to the people in his life. As we proceed, we will explore connections between what we find in Scripture and our own life. The goal is to become more like Jesus.

Our approach will be a *guided discovery.* It will be *guided* because we all need support in understanding Scripture and reflecting on what it means for our lives. Scripture was written to be understood and applied in the community of faith, so we read the Bible *for* ourselves but not *by* ourselves. Even if we are reading alone rather than in a group, we need resources that help us grow in understanding. Our approach is also one of *discovery,* because each of us needs to encounter Scripture for ourselves and consider its meaning for our life. No one can do this for us.

This book is designed to give you both guidance for understanding and tools for discovery.

The introduction on page 6 will guide your reading by providing background material and helping you get oriented to the subject of our exploration. Each week, a brief "Background" section will give you context for the reading, and the "Exploring the Theme" section that follows the reading will bring out the meaning of the Scripture passages. Supplementary material between sessions will offer further resources for understanding.

The main tool for discovery is the "Questions for Reflection and Discussion" section in each session. The first questions in this section are designed to spur you to notice things in the text, sharpen your powers of observation, and read for comprehension. Other questions suggest ways to compare the people, situations, and experiences in the biblical texts with your own life and the world today—an important step toward grasping what God is saying to you through the Scripture and what your response might be. Choose the questions you think will work best for you. Preparing to answer all of the questions ahead of time is highly recommended.

We suggest that you pay particular attention to the final question each week, labeled "Focus question." This question points to an especially important issue raised by the reading. You may find it difficult to answer this focus question briefly. Do leave enough time for everyone in the group to discuss it!

Other sections encourage you to take an active approach to your Bible reading and discussion. At the start of each session, the "Questions to Begin" will help you break the ice and start talk flowing. Often these questions are light and have only a slight connection to the reading. After each Scripture reading, there is a suggested time for a "First Impression." This gives you a chance to express a brief, initial, personal response to the text. Each session ends with a "Prayer to Close" that suggests a way of expressing your response to God.

How long are the discussion sessions? We've assumed you will have about an hour and twenty minutes. If you have less time, you'll find that most of the elements can be shortened somewhat.

Is homework necessary? You will get the most out of your discussions if you read the weekly material and prepare your answers to the questions in advance of each meeting. If participants are not able to prepare, read the "Exploring the Theme" sections aloud at the points where they appear.

What about leadership? You don't have to be an expert in the Bible to lead a discussion. Choose one or two people to act as discussion facilitators, and have everyone in the group read "Suggestions for Bible Discussion Groups" (page 90) before beginning.

Does everyone need a guide? a Bible? Everyone in the group will need their own copy of this book. It contains the biblical texts, so a Bible is not absolutely necessary—but each person will find it useful to have one. You should have at least one Bible on hand for your discussions. (See page 94 for recommendations.)

Before you begin, take a look at the suggestions for Bible discussion groups (page 90) or individuals (page 93).

The Importance of Asking the Right Question

Detroit being the Motor City, some Christians called a press conference in Detroit to launch a media campaign called "What Would Jesus Drive?" They wanted to spur people to reflect on their auto-buying habits in light of the gospel. The organizers of the campaign seemed to promote the idea that the Lord would choose something modestly priced and fuel efficient rather than an expensive, gas-guzzling SUV. This struck me as being rather unlikely. Obviously, if Jesus were in the market for a new vehicle, he would be looking at pickup trucks. How else would a carpenter get his tools and supplies out to the construction site?

Seriously, I'm sure the "What Would Jesus Drive?" folks had good intentions. But their campaign demonstrates the limitations of the What would Jesus do? type of question. Granted, the question is thought provoking. But the answers can range only from speculative to silly. Sometimes the question simply provides an opportunity to communicate a preconceived view. If you dislike SUVs, you picture Jesus driving an Escort.

Jesus calls us to imitate him. This is at the heart of being his followers. But if we wonder what it means to live out his approach to life in our own situations, we usually cannot make much progress simply by asking What would Jesus do?

One reason for this difficulty is that Jesus dealt with situations quite different from ours. Indeed, the whole world in which he lived was different from ours. He was born long, long before the first SUV pulled up to a gas pump, before jets crisscrossed the skies or trains rolled down tracks, before television, or even printing, before effective medical care. In Jesus' day, peasants plowed fields with oxen, and sailing ships plied the seas. Thus the choices that the people of his time faced were different from those we confront. From observing how Jesus lived in his first-century world, it is not easy to determine what he would do if he were suddenly transported into modern life. We know that he went outside of Capernaum to pray one morning (Mark 1:35), but this does not give us a clue as to whether he would use his morning commute to pray in his car or listen to music. When he visited Capernaum, Jesus stayed at Peter's house (Mark 1:29–34); this tells us nothing about whether he would stay in a Motel 6 or a Hilton if he visited Cincinnati.

Another factor that sets a distance between Jesus' life and ours is the difference between his calling and ours. Jesus was called to remain single; most of us are called to marry. He had to leave home to fulfill his mission; most of us establish a home and stay in it. He did not have children of his own; for many of us, raising our children is our great life's work. On a typical day, Jesus cured crowds of sick people. Most of us spend our time in more ordinary activities: earning a living, shopping, hurrying from one activity to another, doing a thousand and one things to keep life together. It is hard to say what Jesus would do if he were suddenly placed in the midst of our activities.

The apostle Paul seems to have already sensed this issue a mere twenty or thirty years after Jesus' resurrection. When he exhorts his fellow Christians to imitate Jesus, he mentions few specifics of Jesus' life. Paul keeps his call to imitate Jesus on a general level. He summons Christians to imitate the overall pattern of Jesus' life—his humble entry into the world as a human being and his supreme service of laying down his life for us (Philippians 2:1–8).

The question What would Jesus do? is not only hard to answer. In some sense, it is the wrong question. In Jesus, God took flesh as a particular individual human being. He was the Son of Mary, he was Jewish, he lived in Nazareth, he spoke Aramaic, he died in Jerusalem. God's plan is not to have Jesus, the first-century Palestinian Jew, step into the billions of situations that develop through human history. His plan is for us, who find ourselves in these varied situations, to live in the Spirit of his Son, to follow his principles for living, to shape our lives according to his values, to share his love with the people around us. The question for each of us is not What would Jesus do? but What does Jesus want me to do? How can each of us, as the particular man or woman we are, be his follower in our situation? Imitating Jesus involves something more complex than simply asking What would Jesus do? It begins with getting to know Jesus and the life he lived, and then translating what we have seen in him into our own lives, according to God's unique call to each of us.

The Gospels provide us with material we need for this process of observation and translation. As one reads the Gospels chapter by chapter, one discovers a very human Jesus—a person in whom his divinity did not replace his humanity in any way. Like every other human being, he was born and grew up. He had a human mind and will. He experienced human pleasures and pressures; he felt human desires, frustrations, and pain. He had a family, he made friends; he loved them and ran into problems with them. Certainly, Jesus lived in a world very different from ours in terms of economy, culture, politics, and religion. Certainly, as the Son of God and Redeemer of the world, he had a unique task in the world, as well as unique power to accomplish it. Still, Jesus fully shared our human nature. As a human being, Jesus is essentially no farther from us than any other human person. The world has changed in twenty centuries, but not human nature.

The Gospels give us access to the human-as-well-as-divine Jesus. They communicate not only his teaching; they narrate more than his death and resurrection. The Gospels consist mostly of short, crisp accounts of episodes in Jesus' public life and in his relationship with his disciples. Thus the Gospels enable us to share the opportunity that Jesus granted to his first disciples— the opportunity to be with him, to observe him and listen to him, to see how he related to people, to learn what it means to be his followers.

In fact, the Gospels are designed to facilitate our interaction with Jesus. They are like video games in which the player steps into a story and interacts with the characters within it. The Gospels invite us not only to observe Jesus but also to step inside his situations and speak with him and listen to him as he speaks to us. In this process, we become acquainted with him as a person. His presence has an impact on our hearts and minds. Through this, we gradually come to see what it means to imitate him, to follow his approach to life, in our circumstances.

This book is an aid to taking advantage of this opportunity. Our particular focus will be to look at how Jesus related to the people in his life. Our aim will be to grow in treating the people in our lives as he would wish us to.

In order to explore the topic, I chose some of the types of people with whom Jesus interacted—the members of his family, those who sought to learn from him, those who opposed him, and others. Then I selected episodes that illustrate his way of relating to each group.

Each week, our format will be the same. In each session you will find three or four excerpts from the Gospels, with a few words of introduction labeled "The Background." After the readings, in "Exploring the Theme," I will offer some help for understanding what is going on in the Gospel episodes, followed by some general reflections on what the accounts show us about Jesus' way of relating to people. At this point, it will be up to you to pick up the ball and run with it. What strikes *you* about the way Jesus relates to people? What picture of Jesus do *you* form from these accounts? What can you learn from him that is relevant for relating to people in *your* life? Each week, the "Questions for Reflection and Discussion" will help you pursue these questions.

Writing this book has been an experience of discovery for me. As I picked out passages from the Gospels, I wondered what I would find out about Jesus' way of dealing with people. As I studied the selections, I was impressed anew with some things I already knew about Jesus. But I also noticed some things for the first time. I hope that, as you read these Gospel passages, you will have the same experience of discovery. Learning about Jesus is an exciting process, even though it involves some hard thinking about how to translate what we see in his life into our lives.

It will be helpful, before we begin, to consider some limitations we will face in our exploration. One limitation is built into the Gospels. Quite simply, there is a lot of Jesus' life that the Gospels do not include. Almost everything in his life before he began his public ministry remains out of sight. The people of Nazareth knew Jesus as the village carpenter. But in the Gospels we never see him working at his trade. Living in a small village, with what may have been a large extended family, Jesus must have been deeply intertwined with relatives and neighbors. But there are no Gospel accounts of Jesus while he was living at home with Mary and Joseph, no stories in which we see him picking olives with his cousins and neighbors, chatting about the weather, visiting a sick neighbor, or listening to his grandparents. It would be interesting to have access to such details, both in order to flesh out our picture of Jesus and to have more material to work with when we try to understand how to imitate him in our family and work lives. But that is not what the Gospel writers have given us.

The Gospels focus on Jesus after he began his public ministry. But even in this period of his life, most of the ordinary moments go unrecorded. Undoubtedly, much of his life was mundane and unremarkable, even after he began his preaching. Presumably, like us, Jesus had downtime when he was too tired to do more than just stare blankly into space (he was exhausted enough to sleep through a life-threatening storm at sea—Mark 4:35–38). No doubt he had to buy new sandals from time to time and get his clothing laundered. Personally, I would like to know how Jesus reacted when people wanted to talk about things that bored him, how he bargained in the bazaar, what kinds of jokes he liked—and told (I do think Jesus had a sense of humor—John 6:5, for example). But, again, the Gospel writers have not informed us.

The Gospel writers' selectivity has given us a portrait that is true, but also partial. By depicting Jesus mainly doing important things, like preaching about the kingdom of God and training his disciples, the authors have created a portrait of him as a serious, even grave, person. We should certainly accept this portrait as true to life. We may, however, suspect that Jesus also had a lighter side. Did he ever ask Levi what he had liked about tax collecting? Did he chat with Andrew about the best places on the lake for fishing? Did he discuss the ups and downs of the fish-drying business with Mary Magdalene (supposing that those scholars are correct who think that was the business in which she made her money)? It seems to me that Jesus must have gotten into ordinary conversations, out of a natural interest in people.

These are just my supposings. But I offer them to spur you to do your own thinking about Jesus. The Gospels are bare-bones accounts; we, the readers, need to flesh them out. As you read the selections from the Gospels over the next few weeks, use your imagination to fill in the sparse picture that the Gospel writers have provided. Create in your mind your own living portrait of Jesus. The more he lives in your mind as a real person, the deeper his influence on you will be.

This book, too, has its limitations. In order to accommodate several Gospel passages in each session, it has been necessary sometimes to read only the parts of incidents that are of particular concern for our investigation. To gain a deeper understanding, you may sometimes wish to pull out your Bible and read the material before and after each excerpt.

Similarly, we will not be able to explore all the layers of meaning in the selections that we read. The Gospels are rich in meaning because Jesus is rich in meaning. The most we can do in a short guide such as this is to *begin* to consider what these passages mean. Hopefully you will go on to read them again and to learn more about them.

For each session's selection of Gospel readings there were more candidates than could be included. For example, in Week 1 we will read about Mary's first appearance in the Gospel of John, at Cana, but we will not read about her appearance later in John's Gospel, at Jesus' cross. Feel free to look for additional passages that would illustrate each week's theme and add them to your reflections.

Despite these limitations, we can be confident that our readings will lead us closer to Jesus. The risen Lord invites us to know him and learn from him. As we ponder how he treated the people in his life, his Spirit will guide us, bringing the stories to life for us and giving us wisdom to see what Jesus' example means for our lives. As we explore how Jesus treated the people in his life, he will help us see how he would like us to treat the people in ours.

Jesus' Way of Relating to His Family

Questions to Begin

10 minutes
Use a question or two to get warmed up for the reading.

1   When you were a child, did you ever get lost? As a parent, have you ever had a child get lost?

2   Do you to prefer to travel alone or with other people? Who do you like to travel with?

What can I do to participate well in the discussion? . . . Stick to the point.

Elizabeth W. Flynn and John F. La Faso, *Group Discussion as Learning Process: A Sourcebook*

*10 minutes
Read the passage aloud. Let individuals take turns reading
paragraphs.*

The Background

We begin our exploration close to home, with Gospel readings that
illustrate Jesus' relationships with members of his family. While
this is a natural starting point for our exploration, it is also in some
ways the most difficult. This is partly because the Gospels show
us virtually nothing of Jesus' family life in Nazareth before he began
his public life and also because, during his public life, Jesus often
had to distance himself from his family in order to pursue the mission
God had given him. Nevertheless, Jesus' values and character come
into very clear focus in his interactions with his family members—
offering us much food for thought about our relationships with our
own families and, indeed, with all the people in our lives.

The Reading: Luke 2:41–52; John 2:1–12; 7:1–10; Mark 3:19–35

A Confrontation with His Parents

Luke 2:41 Now every year his parents went to Jerusalem for the festival
of the Passover. 42 And when he was twelve years old, they went up as
usual for the festival. 43 When the festival was ended and they started
to return, the boy Jesus stayed behind in Jerusalem, but his parents
did not know it. 44 Assuming that he was in the group of travelers,
they went a day's journey. Then they started to look for him among
their relatives and friends. 45 When they did not find him, they returned
to Jerusalem to search for him. 46 After three days they found him in
the temple, sitting among the teachers, listening to them and asking
them questions. 47 And all who heard him were amazed at his
understanding and his answers. 48 When his parents saw him they
were astonished; and his mother said to him, "Child, why have you
treated us like this? Look, your father and I have been searching for
you in great anxiety." 49 He said to them, "Why were you searching
for me? Did you not know that I must be in my Father's house?" 50 But
they did not understand what he said to them. 51 Then he went down
with them and came to Nazareth, and was obedient to them. His
mother treasured all these things in her heart.

^{52} And Jesus increased in wisdom and in years, and in divine and human favor.

A Conversation with His Mother

John 2:1 On the third day there was a wedding in Cana of Galilee, and the mother of Jesus was there. ^{2} Jesus and his disciples had also been invited to the wedding. ^{3} When the wine gave out, the mother of Jesus said to him, "They have no wine." ^{4} And Jesus said to her, "Woman, what concern is that to you and to me? My hour has not yet come." ^{5} His mother said to the servants, "Do whatever he tells you." ^{6} Now standing there were six stone water jars for the Jewish rites of purification, each holding twenty or thirty gallons. ^{7} Jesus said to them, "Fill the jars with water." And they filled them up to the brim. ^{8} He said to them, "Now draw some out, and take it to the chief steward." So they took it.

^{9} When the steward tasted the water that had become wine, and did not know where it came from (though the servants who had drawn the water knew), the steward called the bridegroom ^{10} and said to him, "Everyone serves the good wine first, and then the inferior wine after the guests have become drunk. But you have kept the good wine until now." ^{11} Jesus did this, the first of his signs, in Cana of Galilee, and revealed his glory; and his disciples believed in him.

^{12} After this he went down to Capernaum with his mother, his brothers, and his disciples; and they remained there a few days.

A Disagreement with His Brothers

John 7:1 After this Jesus went about in Galilee. . . . ^{2} Now the Jewish festival of Booths was near. ^{3} So his brothers said to him, "Leave here and go to Judea so that your disciples also may see the works you are doing; ^{4} for no one who wants to be widely known acts in secret. If you do these things, show yourself to the world." ^{5} (For not even his brothers believed in him.)

^{6} Jesus said to them, "My time has not yet come, but your time is always here. ^{7} The world cannot hate you, but it hates me because I testify against it that its works are evil. ^{8} Go to the festival yourselves. I am not going to this festival, for my time has not yet fully come." ^{9} After saying this, he remained in Galilee.

[10] But after his brothers had gone to the festival, then he also went, not publicly but as it were in secret.

A Challenge to Everyone in His Family

Mark 3:19 . . . Then he went home; [20] and the crowd came together again, so that they could not even eat. [21] When his family heard it, they went out to restrain him, for people were saying, "He has gone out of his mind." [22] And the scribes who came down from Jerusalem said, "He has Beelzebul, and by the ruler of the demons he casts out demons." [23] And he called them to him, and spoke to them in parables, "How can Satan cast out Satan? [24] If a kingdom is divided against itself, that kingdom cannot stand. [25] And if a house is divided against itself, that house will not be able to stand. [26] And if Satan has risen up against himself and is divided, he cannot stand, but his end has come. [27] But no one can enter a strong man's house and plunder his property without first tying up the strong man; then indeed the house can be plundered.

[28] "Truly I tell you, people will be forgiven for their sins and whatever blasphemies they utter; [29] but whoever blasphemes against the Holy Spirit can never have forgiveness, but is guilty of an eternal sin"— [30] for they had said, "He has an unclean spirit."

[31] Then his mother and his brothers came; and standing outside, they sent to him and called him. [32] A crowd was sitting around him; and they said to him, "Your mother and your brothers and sisters are outside, asking for you." [33] And he replied, "Who are my mother and my brothers?" [34] And looking at those who sat around him, he said, "Here are my mother and my brothers! [35] Whoever does the will of God is my brother and sister and mother."

First Impression

5 minutes
Briefly mention a question you have about the reading or one thing in it that surprised, impressed, delighted, or challenged you. No discussion! Just listen to one another's reactions.

Exploring the Theme

If participants have not read this section already, read it aloud. Otherwise go on to "Questions for Reflection and Discussion."

Luke 2:41–52. Mary and Joseph set out on the trek from Jerusalem to Nazareth with family members, friends, and neighbors. Perhaps the caravan is large, and Mary and Joseph are busy socializing. In any case, they do not notice that Jesus is not with the group until they stop to camp for the night. What can have happened to him? The next day they hurriedly return to Jerusalem. The following day they find him in the temple. Luke tells us they are "astonished." Apparently Jesus is normally a compliant and responsible boy who does not give his parents a hard time. "Child, why have you treated us like this?" Mary asks. "Look, your father and I have been searching for you in great anxiety" (2:48).

Yet Jesus does not apologize. In fact, he reproaches Mary and Joseph in public for not knowing his whereabouts! The Greek text of verse 50 contains a hint that he *had* told them before they left town but they had not grasped his meaning. Nevertheless, he tells them, even if they do not understand—even if it makes them anxious—he must be in his Father's house, doing his Father's business (2:49). Jesus' reference to his Father expresses his deep awareness of his identity and mission: he is the Son of God, he has come to carry out his Father's will—and only his Father's will. This point is so important that he is willing to trouble and embarrass his parents in order to help them grasp it.

Having made his point, Jesus is again submissive to Joseph and Mary (2:51). The submission of the Son of God as an ordinary teenager to human parents is quite remarkable. But putting his Father's will first does not make Jesus a rebel without a cause.

John 2:1–12. In first-century Galilee, wedding festivities last seven days. Guests are expected to bring supplies for the lengthy celebration, which may account for Mary's bringing the wine problem to Jesus' attention. "We helped to drink up the wine. Shouldn't we do something to replenish it?"

Jesus, however, is somewhat aloof. "Woman" is a polite form of address but an odd way for a son to address his mother. Jesus' question—"what concern is that to you and to me?"—is a way of saying, "That's your business. How am I involved?" By saying that his "hour" (2:4—his death and resurrection) has not yet come, Jesus reminds his mother that he must act in accord with his Father's plans—plans that he alone fully understands. Mary's direction to the servants (2:5), then, is an act of faith in Jesus in the absence of complete understanding, which makes her a good model for us. Yet, as St. Francis de Sales points out, Mary's instruction to the servants indicates that she is mysteriously in tune with her son, since she knows he is going to tell the servants to do something.

Jesus' miracle signifies that God's dealings with the people of Israel (symbolized by the water jars used for ritual washings under the Mosaic law) have been a preparation for the coming of the Son, whose arrival can now be celebrated (symbolized by the wine). Jesus has granted his mother's unspoken request, but only after making it clear that he owes a son's obedience to one person alone—his heavenly Father.

John 7:1–10. Jesus' "brothers" (see essay, page 84) believe in him in the sense of recognizing that he can do marvelous things. But they do not *really* believe in him: they do not grasp what his miracles signify—that he is God's life-giving Son. To his brothers, Jesus seems to be just an ordinary family member who has unaccountably developed extraordinary powers.

The brothers expect a spiritually gifted person like Jesus to use his powers to impress people and gain honor for himself and his family. So they urge him to go to the big city and show off (7:3–4). Jesus refuses the suggestion on the basis of God's plan (7:6). And he rebukes his brothers by telling them, "You don't have to ask God about his timing because you do whatever you want. So any time seems good to you." After a delay, Jesus does go to Jerusalem (7:10), but not for the reason his brothers propose. On this trip, he will perform no miracles.

Mark 3:19–35. Jesus' "home" here is not the family residence in Nazareth. Probably he is staying in Capernaum (see Mark 1:21, 29). Members of his family have heard rumors that he has gone insane. Apparently they give credence to the rumors, for they come to "restrain" him (the Greek word means "seize" or "arrest," which is how it is used in Mark 14:46). Presumably they want to take charge of him for his own good and to preserve the family's good name. (Did his mother also? Again, see page 84.) The religious authorities accuse Jesus of demonic possession— a diagnosis that overlaps with insanity in ancient thinking (see John 10:20).

The episode ends with a picture of insiders and outsiders (3:31–35). Inside the house are Jesus' disciples, receiving his teaching about God and experiencing his power to overcome evil and forgive sins. Outside are those who do not believe in him. The outsiders can become insiders by believing. If they believe, they will enjoy a closeness to him as intimate as that between sister and brother and between mother and child. But those who belong to Jesus' natural family are not necessarily close to him. Unless they believe in him, they will remain outside.

Reflections. Jesus' calling in life did not involve marriage, so obviously we do not find Gospel incidents in which he is surrounded by a family of his own. But we know that he was deeply committed to family life: he opposed divorce, he liked children, he insisted on adults caring for their elderly parents, (Mark 10:1–16; 7:9–13). So we might expect to see him tightening the bonds between himself and his family members. Instead, we repeatedly see him drawing a line between himself and his family. In one situation after another, he lets them feel as though they have bumped up against an invisible barrier between themselves and him. Why is this?

Family relationships were very strong in first-century Palestine. A person tended to think of himself or herself not as an independent individual but as part of a family. Consequently, people were deeply influenced by their family's expectations for them. To the extent that Jesus' family members did not grasp his identity and wished him to act in ways not in keeping with his mission, these close family bonds would have been a problem for him. The numerous incidents in the Gospels where we see Jesus distancing himself from his family suggest that he felt it necessary to make clear to his family that he would not let his ties with them hold him back from doing exactly what his Father wanted him to do.

Undoubtedly, Jesus was confrontational with his family
for their good. His brothers needed sharp words to jolt them
into realizing who he was (eventually some of them became his
followers—see page 89). Perhaps also Jesus was confrontational
with his family because he found it necessary for himself. As a
first-century Palestinian Jew who loved his family deeply, he must
have felt the pull of their expectations. Perhaps his brothers'
suggestion to win renown through his miracles appealed to him.
Their proposal was similar to the suggestion of the devil in the
desert, which seems to have been a genuine temptation for him
(Matthew 4:5–7; Luke 4:9–12). Jesus' sharp words to his brothers
may have been a way of being stern with himself, reaffirming his
rejection of values and goals that did not come from his Father.

Our readings show Jesus repeatedly expressing his
determination to put obedience to God before even his closest
personal relationships. The divergence between his mission and
his family's expectations would have become most apparent
during the period of his ministry. During his earlier years, however,
obedience to his Father would have been expressed mainly through
obedience to his earthly parents. Presumably, also, he showed his
love for God by being a loyal and caring grandson, nephew, cousin.
We catch only a glimpse of this period of his life in Luke's Gospel
(Luke 2:51–52). Yet for most of us, this at-home aspect of Jesus'
relationship with his family is the part that would have been most
like our own. We might wish the Gospel writers had shown us a
little more of it!

In any case, the Gospels show us Jesus applying to
his family relationships the fundamental principle that he calls
us to apply to our own: putting God's will ahead of every other
consideration. Occasionally this may require us to part ways
with our families in some respect. More often, it means just the
opposite. Putting God's will first usually means staying close to
our families, serving them with kindness and determination, no
matter how great the difficulties.

Questions for Reflection and Discussion

45 minutes
Choose questions according to your interest and time.

1 Jesus' words in Luke 2:49 can be translated as meaning either that he must be in his Father's house or about his Father's business. How different are these two possible meanings?

2 Judging from Mary's astonishment and reproach of Jesus (Luke 2:48), he must normally have been a cooperative and thoughtful boy. So, when Mary and Joseph discovered his absence from the caravan (Luke 2:44), what explanation might have occurred to them?

3 Jesus rejects his brothers' encouragement to exhibit his remarkable powers in Jerusalem (John 7:3–4). Since Jesus had "revealed his glory" at Cana by using his miraculous powers (John 2:11), what was wrong with his brothers' advice?

4 How common is it for a person to be misunderstood even by close family members? What causes such misunderstandings? What can be done to overcome misunderstandings in the family? What can be learned from Jesus' way of handling his relationships with family members who do not understand him?

5   Jesus deals with misunderstandings and disagreements directly, even bluntly. How useful is this in family relationships? Is it always the best approach?

6   For personal reflection: Jesus puts obedience to God at the center of his relationships with members of his family. If you gave higher priority to God's will, how might you change the way you relate to someone in your family? How might you do something different from what your family expects?

7   **Focus question:** In what ways do family expectations today help people see and do what God is calling them to? In what ways can family expectations be an obstacle? What can be done to build a family life that encourages all the family members to seek God's will for their lives?

Prayer to Close

10 minutes
Use this approach—or create your own!

◆ Pray this prayer together. Pause for silent reflection. End with an Our Father, a Hail Mary, and a Glory Be.

Lord Jesus, you made obedience to your Father the rock on which you built your relationships with everyone in your family. Help me do the same in my family. Enable me to love with your love. Give me wisdom for dealing with misunderstanding and conflict. Bless every member of my family with a deep knowledge of you.

Saints in the Making

A Conflict in the Family

This section is a supplement for individual reading.

Catherine Benincasa was only in her early teens, but in medieval Siena, Italy, she was old enough to begin preparing for marriage. Her mother, Lapa, wanted her to dress a bit more fashionably, in expectation of visits by young men who met the family's standards for a husband. Catherine, however, felt called to God in a way that made marriage seem like a detour. Her cooperation with her family's marriage preparation program was minimal.

As her mother's pressure on her increased, Catherine dramatized her resistance by cutting off her hair. To her parents, this seemed like craziness. They ordered her to work as a maid in the house. Perhaps if she had less time to sit in her room praying she would learn to be reasonable. Deprived of quiet hours for prayer, Catherine mentally constructed a chapel in her heart. As she cooked and washed floors, she entered a sphere of silence within herself and conversed with Jesus.

Finally, Catherine brought the conflict into the open. One evening, as the family relaxed together after dinner, she announced that she had made a decision as a child to remain single so as to be wed to Jesus. Now the family faced a decision, she said. They could accept her as she was or throw her out. Either way, she was going to respond to God's call.

Her declaration brought some of her brothers and sisters to tears. After a pause, her father, Giacomo, gave his response. "God forbid, my dear daughter, that we should in any way contradict the divine will, from which, as we all realize, comes your holy intention." To the rest of the family he said, "From now on let no one annoy this dearest daughter of mine. Let her serve her Spouse as she wishes, and may she pray for us."

Catherine's relationship with her family did not suddenly become smooth after this. But her parents and siblings gradually came to appreciate her faithfulness to her call. So did Italy, for Catherine ended up acting as peacemaker in some of the most serious political conflicts of her day. After her death, she was proclaimed a saint. The Benincasa family had no idea that any of this would happen. They did know, however, how hard it can be to support a family member in responding to God's call.

. . . TO SEEKERS

Questions to Begin

10 minutes
Use a question or two to get warmed up for the reading.

1 If you could make one thing in life easier, what would it be?

2 When do you especially *not* like to be asked questions?

Who can grasp all the riches of a single one of your words, O Lord?

St. Ephrem

10 minutes
Read the passage aloud. Let individuals take turns reading
paragraphs.

The Background

With miraculous powers, Jesus has been healing large numbers of people. This leads some to believe that he may have been sent by God. One person who reaches this conclusion is a religious scholar named Nicodemus, who visits Jesus in our first reading. For at least one observer, however, Jesus' healings present a problem. John the Baptist preached a fiery judgment to come; he expected that the one who came after him would carry it out. Now Jesus is healing people—which is fine with John—but not bringing judgment. At the time of our reading, John has been arrested (Luke 3:19–20). From his jail cell he sends some of his disciples to Jesus with a question. In our third reading, a third seeker asks a question not about God's plans for the world but merely about his own life. Finally, another religious scholar appears, asking a theological question. Few of us have people coming to us and asking for answers to life's basic questions. But many people around us ponder these questions. What can we learn from Jesus about how to help them find the answers in him?

The Reading: John 2:23–3:16; Luke 7:18–23; Mark 10:17–22; 12:28–34

From Zero to Sixty in Sixteen Verses

John 2:23 When he was in Jerusalem during the Passover festival, many believed in his name because they saw the signs that he was doing. 24 But Jesus on his part would not entrust himself to them, because he knew all people 25 and needed no one to testify about anyone; for he himself knew what was in everyone.

3:1 Now there was a Pharisee named Nicodemus, a leader of the Jews. 2 He came to Jesus by night and said to him, "Rabbi, we know that you are a teacher who has come from God; for no one can do these signs that you do apart from the presence of God." 3 Jesus answered him, "Very truly, I tell you, no one can see the kingdom of God without being born from above." 4 Nicodemus said to him,

"How can anyone be born after having grown old? Can one enter a second time into the mother's womb and be born?" 5 Jesus answered, "Very truly, I tell you, no one can enter the kingdom of God without being born of water and Spirit. 6 What is born of the flesh is flesh, and what is born of the Spirit is spirit.* 7 Do not be astonished that I said to you, 'You must be born from above.' 8 The wind* blows where it chooses, and you hear the sound of it, but you do not know where it comes from or where it goes. So it is with everyone who is born of the Spirit." 9 Nicodemus said to him, "How can these things be?" 10 Jesus answered him, "Are you a teacher of Israel, and yet you do not understand these things?

11 "Very truly, I tell you, we speak of what we know and testify to what we have seen; yet you do not receive our testimony. 12 If I have told you about earthly things and you do not believe, how can you believe if I tell you about heavenly things? 13 No one has ascended into heaven except the one who descended from heaven, the Son of Man. 14 And just as Moses lifted up the serpent in the wilderness, so must the Son of Man be lifted up, 15 that whoever believes in him may have eternal life.

16 "For God so loved the world that he gave his only Son, so that everyone who believes in him may not perish but may have eternal life."

The Answer Is Yes

Luke 7:18 The disciples of John reported all these things to him. So John summoned two of his disciples 19 and sent them to the Lord to ask, "Are you the one who is to come, or are we to wait for another?"

20 When the men had come to him, they said, "John the Baptist has sent us to you to ask, 'Are you the one who is to come, or are we to wait for another?'"

21 Jesus had just then cured many people of diseases, plagues, and evil spirits, and had given sight to many who were blind. 22 And he answered them, "Go and tell John what you have seen and heard: the blind receive their sight, the lame walk, the lepers are cleansed, the deaf hear, the dead are raised, the poor have good news brought to them. 23 And blessed is anyone who takes no offense at me."

*The same Greek word means both "wind" and "spirit."

A Shocking Invitation

Mark 10:17 As he was setting out on a journey, a man ran up and knelt before him, and asked him, "Good Teacher, what must I do to inherit eternal life?" 18 Jesus said to him, "Why do you call me good? No one is good but God alone. 19 You know the commandments: 'You shall not murder; You shall not commit adultery; You shall not steal; You shall not bear false witness; You shall not defraud; Honor your father and mother.'" 20 He said to him, "Teacher, I have kept all these since my youth." 21 Jesus, looking at him, loved him and said, "You lack one thing; go, sell what you own, and give the money to the poor, and you will have treasure in heaven; then come, follow me." 22 When he heard this, he was shocked and went away grieving, for he had many possessions.

Close to the Kingdom

Mark 12:28 One of the scribes came near and heard them disputing with one another, and seeing that he answered them well, he asked him, "Which commandment is the first of all?" 29 Jesus answered, "The first is, 'Hear, O Israel: the Lord our God, the Lord is one; 30 you shall love the Lord your God with all your heart, and with all your soul, and with all your mind, and with all your strength.' 31 The second is this, 'You shall love your neighbor as yourself.' There is no other commandment greater than these." 32 Then the scribe said to him, "You are right, Teacher; you have truly said that 'he is one, and besides him there is no other'; 33 and 'to love him with all the heart, and with all the understanding, and with all the strength,' and 'to love one's neighbor as oneself,'—this is much more important than all whole burnt offerings and sacrifices." 34 When Jesus saw that he answered wisely, he said to him, "You are not far from the kingdom of God."

First Impression

5 minutes
Briefly mention a question you have about the reading or one thing in it that surprised, impressed, delighted, or challenged you. No discussion! Just listen to one another's reactions.

Exploring the Theme

If participants have not read this section already, read it aloud.
Otherwise go on to "Questions for Reflection and Discussion."

John 2:23–3:16. It is night when Jesus welcomes Nicodemus
to the house where he is staying in Jerusalem. Jesus invites his
guest to take a seat in a room dimly lit by an oil lamp. All seems
peaceful—but Nicodemus had better fasten his seat belt. Jesus is
about to take him for a high-speed theological ride.

Jesus assumes that Nicodemus has heard his preaching of
the kingdom of God and wishes to learn more about it, so he gets
right to the point. He tells Nicodemus how people can enter God's
kingdom (3:3). Jesus sometimes uses a technique of misunderstanding: he makes a statement his listener is likely to misinterpret in
order to spur the listener to ask further questions. Jesus uses this
technique here by describing entry into God's kingdom as a birth.
Predictably, Nicodemus misunderstands (3:4). He thinks Jesus
means a physical birth. But Jesus is thinking of a spiritual birth—
either a birth from heaven or a spiritual second birth (the Greek
word translated "from above" may also be translated "anew").
Judging from John 1:12–13, Jesus primarily means a birth from
above, that is, a new existence stemming from God's power rather
than from human ability.

Jesus gives Nicodemus a clue to his meaning by speaking
of "water and Spirit." This should remind Nicodemus of God's
promises in Scripture to cleanse and transform people by water
and Spirit (Ezekiel 36:25–27). Jesus immediately points out that
this action of God's Spirit in human hearts is too great for human
beings to understand (3:8). Nicodemus needs to accept the fact
that God is going to do something that goes far beyond what
Nicodemus can comprehend. In effect, Jesus is saying, "Nicodemus,
you can't understand it, but you can experience it. Come and see."

Struggling to keep up with Jesus' rapid exposition of the
mysterious action of the Spirit, Nicodemus cries out, "I don't get it!"
(see 3:9). He probably reasons that the Spirit has been promised for
the end times, but the end times have not arrived—at least as far
as he can see—so why is Jesus speaking about the gift of the Spirit?

With a bit of sarcasm, Jesus chides Nicodemus for not
understanding (3:10). He wants Nicodemus to recognize his
ignorance so that he will rely on Jesus' instruction. Then Jesus

clearly states the reason why everyone should listen to him: he is the *only* person with insider knowledge of God (3:13). This astounding revelation probably leaves Nicodemus more perplexed than ever. What about Moses, he probably wonders?

Instead of slowing down to deal with Nicodemus's perplexity, Jesus speeds on to another mystery: he will be "lifted up" (3:14). By this, Jesus means not only that he will be lifted up to a shameful death on a cross but that this death will lift him up in glory by fully revealing God's love for the world. Through being lifted up, Jesus will become the means by which men and women enter eternal life with God (3:14–15). This is God's desire for all human beings (3:16). In a short, breathtaking conversation, Jesus has brought Nicodemus to the core of the Creator's plan for the world.

Luke 7:18–23. John the Baptist predicted that someone greater than himself would soon appear. He seems to have expected a figure like the prophet Elijah, bringing the day of God's judgment (Malachi 3:1–5; 4:5; Luke 3:15–17). John probably thinks that Jesus is, in some way, Elijah returned. But Jesus is not fulfilling John's expectations for judgment. Instead of overthrowing oppressors and putting an end to injustices, Jesus is forgiving sins and healing the sick (Luke 5:17–26; 7:1–17). John wonders if he has made a mistake in identifying Jesus as the "one who is to come" (7:20).

In response to John's questions, Jesus shows John's messengers that he is indeed performing merciful miracles, just as John has heard. He alludes to prophecies from Isaiah that speak of God's healing and judgment (see Isaiah 29:18–21; 35:4–6; 61:1–2)—but omits any reference to judgment. In effect, Jesus' answer to John is, "You heard right. I'm bringing God's blessings, not God's judgment. Can you deal with that?" Jesus has not given John an explanation. Rather, he has challenged John to ponder more deeply the mystery that already puzzles him.

Mark 10:17–22. Perhaps the rich man is a genuinely good person who just does not crave perfection. But, as scholar C. E. B. Cranfield points out, "The fact that the man goes away with darkened countenance is the sign that he has made his riches into an idol, from which it is too hard to part." The man goes away "grieving" because he is caught in a struggle between two desires—love of God and love of money. Despite the man's obedience to the commandments, something else has begun to replace God in his heart. Money has become a false god for him, demanding to be served. God *alone* is "good," as Jesus says (10:18), but the rich man is not letting God alone be the good for which he lives.

In 10:21, Jesus does not suggest that the man has earned eternal life by keeping the commandments but can now gain something extra by becoming his disciple. The "one thing" the man lacks is not some spiritual enhancement, a piece of optional equipment for his spiritual life. The one thing he lacks is the one thing that is essential—wholehearted devotion to God. Jesus offers the man something he *needs*—freedom from the false god that enslaves him, peace for his troubled heart. Jesus offers the man the opportunity to keep the first commandment: to love God above all. Out of love ("Jesus, looking at him, loved him"—10:21), Jesus offers to be the bridge on which the man can cross over from his conflicted life into wholehearted devotion to God.

To avail himself of the offer, the man must renounce his false god (by giving away his money) and focus his life on God (by following Jesus). Jesus sets the offer before the man and waits to see what choice he will make.

Mark 12:28–34. Jesus treats the scribe as a sincere seeker of the truth and gives him a straight answer. In response, the scribe shows humility and openness to God. Seeing this, Jesus encourages him: "You are not far from the kingdom of God" (12:34). Indeed! If only the scribe would realize it, he is standing in the presence of the one who is bringing God's kingdom into the world.

Reflections. Jesus seems always to have been available to people who sought him out. Whether he was at home at night, walking along the road, or standing around in the plaza of the temple, he was always ready for a serious conversation about God. Jesus had a clear sense of his mission in life—making God known—and he was always ready to carry it out.

Jesus also seems to have been perceptive about whether people were open to him (John 2:24–25). As we will see in later readings (Week 5), he was reserved toward those who asked him questions only to trap him. But when he sensed that a person wanted to learn, he was lavish with his attention. Jesus rewarded Nicodemus's searching with one of the most profound statements ever made about God's love for the human race (John 3:16). The individualized responses that Jesus gave to those who sought him out show how concerned he was about each person's needs. He looked at the rich man with love (Mark 10:21) and gave him an invitation—sell all and give to the poor—tailored to his particular inner struggle. If the man's idol had been sex or power or fame, Jesus would probably have recommended a different course of action.

While he was always available, Jesus did not always make things easy for those who sought him out. His answers to Nicodemus and John the Baptist must have left them scratching their heads in bewilderment. He advised the rich man to take a very difficult step. Jesus knew that God's ways are not easy for human beings to grasp or respond to. Yet Jesus offered his presence to help them. He mingled encouragement with challenge. "You're close to the kingdom of God," he told the scribe. "Keep going! You'll get there!"

While Jesus calls each of us to cooperate with him in bringing God's kingdom in the world, our roles are necessarily different from his. None of us can say to another person, "Come, follow me!" Yet there is much we can learn from Jesus' way of relating to Nicodemus and the other seekers in these readings. Jesus has a crystal clear sense of the work his Father has entrusted to him—and he is always on task. He has a special love for each person he meets.

Questions for Reflection and Discussion

45 minutes
Choose questions according to your interest and time.

1 Some scholars think that John 3:4 contains a clue as to Nicodemus's age. What do you think?

2 When Jesus recites commandments for the rich man (Mark 10:19), why doesn't he include the two that he later tells the scribe are the most important (Mark 12:29–31)? (There is no one correct answer.)

3 Jesus tells the scribe that he is close to God's kingdom (Mark 12:32–34). Apparently the scribe's answer implied something about God's kingdom. What might that be?

4 Treating people individually, on the basis of their particular situations and needs, involves knowing them. How can a person grow in knowing the people they live with and work with and meet in the course of a day? How could you make a greater effort to get to know some of the people you deal with?

5 Jesus confronted Nicodemus and John the Baptist with mysteries concerning himself and God's plan of salvation.

What has given you a sense of the mysteriousness of God and his ways? Do you take time to reflect on these mysteries? What has helped you grow in understanding them?

6 For personal reflection: Reread Mark 10:17–22 as the description of a conversation between Jesus and you. Fill it out and adjust it to make it closer to what an actual conversation between Jesus and you might be like. Reflect on what the conversation reveals about you and how Jesus is calling you to respond to him.

7 Focus question: Jesus seems to have had a clear idea of his mission in the world and to have been always ready to carry it out. How can a person get a sense of God's purposes for his or her life? How do the ordinary aspects of life—work, family life, recreation, and so on—fit into a person's God-given mission in life? What mission has God entrusted to you? How could you grow in carrying it out?

Prayer to Close

10 minutes
Use this approach—or create your own!

◆ Use Nicodemus's question (John 3:9) in a litany of petition. After each of the following prayers, pray, "Lord, how can these things be?" At the end, pause for silent reflection and conclude with an Our Father.

Lord Jesus, you offer us a share in your own life in the Spirit.

Lord, how can these things be?

You promise to make us new by the power of your Spirit.

Lord, how can these things be?

You have given your life on the cross so that we might live with you forever.

Lord, how can these things be?

You ask us to leave behind everything that turns our hearts away from you.

Lord, how can these things be?

You call us to share in your love for the Father and for the people around us.

Lord, how can these things be?

Saints in the Making

Learning to Speak Up

This section is a supplement for individual reading.

When it comes to talking with people who want to know God better, a difference between Jesus and most of his followers stands out pretty clearly: Jesus was always ready; most of us usually aren't. Probably many of us are reluctant to get into conversations about God because we feel we are not equipped to do an adequate job of communication.

Many of us accept this deficiency as unchangeable—a kind of inherited disability. Every once in a while, however, some Christians try to do something about it. "Look," they say, "lots of people would like to know God better and have a deeper relationship with him—and they would be interested in talking with us about God, if we knew how to do it. So, let's learn how."

A group of English Catholics took this approach in the early twentieth century. Laypeople, with a few priests, organized a speaking society called the Catholic Evidence Guild in London in 1918. They took turns giving short talks on Catholicism and answering questions in public places, such as parks. Behind their open-air speaking, they developed an extensive training program "to educate themselves in the Catholic faith and learn how to communicate about it effectively. Before members stood up on a street corner to speak as a member of the group, they had to pass through a rigorous training program. This involved reading, listening to other speakers, and participating in practice speaking sessions with critiques from fellow members. Two leaders of the group, Frank Sheed and Maisie Ward, produced a training manual that provided outlines for talks and lists of sample questions that speakers should be prepared for. The Catholic Evidence Guild was convinced that ordinary Catholics *can* learn enough about their faith to communicate it to others effectively. The participants did not become professional theologians, but many of them did become effective communicators of the Catholic faith.

The guild spread in England and the United States in the 1920s and 1930s. It became inactive in the United States in the 1970s, but a small group revived the New York chapter in the 1990s and began anew the process of learning to share the gospel on the street.

. . . to Those Known as Sinners

Questions to Begin

10 minutes
Use a question or two to get warmed up for the reading.

1 What is your favorite fragrance (flower, perfume, lotion, whatever)?

2 When have you been glad that someone stood up for you against another person's criticism?

If you are an active reader, the biblical texts have the power to speak to your personal mentality, to quicken it, to spring surprises, to expose and terminate illusions.

H. A. Nielsen, *The Bible—As If for the First Time*

Opening the Bible

10 minutes
Read the passage aloud. Let individuals take turns reading
paragraphs.

The Background

In our readings this week, most of us are on familiar ground. Here
we see that Jesus is merciful to sinners—possibly his best-known
characteristic. The challenge in exploring this week's readings is
to learn *how* he expresses his mercy and how his mercy goes along
with his call to live rightly. In our four readings, Jesus speaks with
two men and two women who are considered to be big sinners. In
two cases we are told their sins—one is a toll collector (implication:
an extortionist), the other is an adulterer. In the other two cases
we are not told the nature of their sins. Of course, there are more
than four sinners in these readings. With the exception of Jesus,
everyone in the stories is a sinner. But whether everyone realizes
this is a question that runs throughout these incidents. What do
we learn here about how Jesus relates to us? about how he wishes
us to relate to other people?

The Reading: Luke 5:27–32; 7:36–50; John 8:2–11; Luke 23:32–43

Levi's Banquet

Luke 5:27 After this he went out and saw a tax collector named Levi,
sitting at the tax booth; and he said to him, "Follow me." 28 And he
got up, left everything, and followed him.

29 Then Levi gave a great banquet for him in his house; and
there was a large crowd of tax collectors and others sitting at the
table with them. 30 The Pharisees and their scribes were complaining
to his disciples, saying, "Why do you eat and drink with tax collectors
and sinners?" 31 Jesus answered, "Those who are well have no need
of a physician, but those who are sick; 32 I have come to call not the
righteous but sinners to repentance."

Simon's Banquet

Luke 7:36 One of the Pharisees asked Jesus to eat with him, and he went
into the Pharisee's house and took his place at the table. 37 And a

woman in the city, who was a sinner, having learned that he was eating in the Pharisee's house, brought an alabaster jar of ointment. 38 She stood behind him at his feet, weeping, and began to bathe his feet with her tears and to dry them with her hair. Then she continued kissing his feet and anointing them with the ointment. 39 Now when the Pharisee who had invited him saw it, he said to himself, "If this man were a prophet, he would have known who and what kind of woman this is who is touching him—that she is a sinner." 40 Jesus spoke up and said to him, "Simon, I have something to say to you." "Teacher," he replied, "speak." 41 "A certain creditor had two debtors; one owed five hundred denarii, and the other fifty. 42 When they could not pay, he canceled the debts for both of them. Now which of them will love him more?" 43 Simon answered, "I suppose the one for whom he canceled the greater debt." And Jesus said to him, "You have judged rightly." 44 Then turning toward the woman, he said to Simon, "Do you see this woman? I entered your house; you gave me no water for my feet, but she has bathed my feet with her tears and dried them with her hair. 45 You gave me no kiss, but from the time I came in she has not stopped kissing my feet. 46 You did not anoint my head with oil, but she has anointed my feet with ointment. 47 Therefore, I tell you, her sins, which were many, have been forgiven; hence she has shown great love. But the one to whom little is forgiven, loves little." 48 Then he said to her, "Your sins are forgiven." 49 But those who were at the table with him began to say among themselves, "Who is this who even forgives sins?" 50 And he said to the woman, "Your faith has saved you; go in peace."

An Accusation in the Temple

John 8:2 Early in the morning he came again to the temple. All the people came to him and he sat down and began to teach them. 3 The scribes and the Pharisees brought a woman who had been caught in adultery; and making her stand before all of them, 4 they said to him, "Teacher, this woman was caught in the very act of committing adultery. 5 Now in the law Moses commanded us to stone such women. Now what do you say?" 6 They said this to test him, so that they might have some charge to bring against him. Jesus bent down and wrote with his finger on the ground. 7 When they kept on questioning him, he straightened up and said to them, "Let anyone among you who is without sin be the first to throw a stone at her." ⁸ And once again he bent down and wrote on the ground. ⁹ When they heard it, they went away, one by one, beginning with the elders; and Jesus was left alone with the woman standing before him. ¹⁰ Jesus straightened up and said to her, "Woman, where are they? Has no one condemned you?" ¹¹ She said, "No one, sir." And Jesus said, "Neither do I condemn you. Go your way, and from now on do not sin again."

A Conversation among Three Dying Men

Luke 23:32 Two others also, who were criminals, were led away to be put to death with him. ³³ When they came to the place that is called The Skull, they crucified Jesus there with the criminals, one on his right and one on his left. ³⁴ Then Jesus said, "Father, forgive them; for they do not know what they are doing." And they cast lots to divide his clothing.

³⁵ And the people stood by, watching; but the leaders scoffed at him, saying, "He saved others; let him save himself if he is the Messiah of God, his chosen one!" ³⁶ The soldiers also mocked him, coming up and offering him sour wine, ³⁷ and saying, "If you are the King of the Jews, save yourself!" ³⁸ There was also an inscription over him, "This is the King of the Jews."

³⁹ One of the criminals who were hanged there kept deriding him and saying, "Are you not the Messiah? Save yourself and us!"

⁴⁰ But the other rebuked him, saying, "Do you not fear God, since you are under the same sentence of condemnation? ⁴¹ And we indeed have been condemned justly, for we are getting what we deserve for our deeds, but this man has done nothing wrong." ⁴² Then he said, "Jesus, remember me when you come into your kingdom."

⁴³ He replied, "Truly I tell you, today you will be with me in Paradise."

First Impression

5 minutes
Briefly mention a question you have about the reading or one thing in it that surprised, impressed, delighted, or challenged you. No discussion! Just listen to one another's reactions.

Exploring the Theme

If participants have not read this section already, read it aloud.
Otherwise go on to "Questions for Reflection and Discussion."

Luke 5:27–32. Levi collects tolls at a booth alongside a road where people transport goods. He is probably an independent contractor who holds a toll-collecting franchise from the government. As a toll collector he makes a living by demanding more—sometimes a lot more—from the people who are moving goods than the government demands from him. Soldiers put muscle behind his demands (see Luke 3:12–14). Squeezing money out of farmers and business people pushes up the prices of basic commodities. This makes life harder for everyone, especially the poor. No surprise: toll collectors are unpopular. Many people regard them as enemies of society.

About Levi in particular we know little besides his name—but his name tells us something. His parents named him after one of the ancestors of the tribes of Israel. Since these ancestors' names were popular among pious Jews in the time of Jesus, Levi may have grown up in a religious environment. Later, though, he turned away from the values and lifestyle he learned at home. Now, Jesus is leading him back into the community of faith.

In first-century Palestine, sharing a meal expresses a personal relationship. By attending Levi's banquet, Jesus signifies that he has a relationship with Levi and other toll collectors. Some of the Pharisees and scribes are appalled. Is it because they think Jesus is soft on sin? Perhaps. But elsewhere Jesus clearly shows that his moral standards are high (see Luke 6:36). He opposes extortion as much as anyone else (see Luke 20:46–47).

Are Jesus' opponents angry at him because he wishes to heal the souls of toll collectors (5:30–32)? Do the Pharisees and scribes deny the possibility of repentance and rehabilitation? Probably not. More likely they would be glad to see Levi and his crowd give up their dishonest practices—for everyone's sake. They might even welcome repentant toll collectors back into the community—*after* they go to the temple, offer sacrifices, and change their way of life. What offends the religious leaders is that Jesus is socializing with toll collectors *while they are still sinners.*

Here we see two diametrically opposed ways of dealing with sinners and sin. The Pharisees shun big-time sinners as a way of showing disapproval of their behavior. Jesus associates with sinners as a way of leading them to repentance. The Pharisees use social pressure; Jesus uses personal presence.

Take Levi, for example. When Jesus calls Levi to follow him, there is no indication that Levi instantly reevaluates his entire life and repents of all his extortions. He simply decides to leave his work and spend time with Jesus. He does what the rich man in last week's reading refused to do. Hopefully, Levi's decision will launch him into a process of repentance: as he gets to know Jesus, he will come to see himself in a new light and decide to live in a better manner. As for the other toll collectors at Levi's party, they do not seem to have checked *their* sins at the door. Yet Jesus has dinner with them anyway.

Luke 7:36–50. Now Jesus is dining at the home of one of the religious experts, a Pharisee named Simon. Simon is open to the possibility that Jesus is a prophet (see 7:39).

At first-century banquets, guests recline on couches facing toward the center of the room. During this meal, a woman enters the dining room and stands at Jesus' feet, behind him. Simon recognizes her as "a sinner." He probably knows what sins she has committed, but Luke does not pass on that information to us. The woman begins to weep. Perhaps she feels remorse for her sins. Or perhaps she is crying from joy at having received forgiveness from Jesus. Perhaps she is receiving forgiveness at this very moment.

Jesus does not defend the woman against Simon's unspoken criticism. The parable does not imply that the woman is not a sinner. Rather, it invites Simon to ask himself whether he isn't a sinner also.

Apparently, Jesus thinks Simon needs some stronger medicine than the parable provides. So he compares the treatment he received from the woman and from Simon (7:44–46). The comparison is two-edged. By publicly acknowledging the woman's kindness to him, Jesus honors her, thus encouraging the other guests to accept her back into the community of faith. At the same time, the comparison shames Simon in front of his guests. Jesus is not expressing resentment at Simon's less-than-generous hospitality (Simon has neglected some nice touches, but by the standards of the time he has not been a bad host). Jesus wants

Simon to consider *why* he has not been more hospitable. Does Simon love little because he has experienced little forgiveness? If so, is this because he doesn't need much forgiveness—or because he is unwilling to acknowledge his need? Or is Simon blind to his sins?

Since the woman needs no correction or criticism to make her aware of her sins, Jesus gives her none. He simply reassures her that she has been forgiven and gives her a blessing (7:48–50).

John 8:2–11. The woman's accusers present Jesus with a dilemma. If he favors leniency, he will be rejecting the Mosaic law, which calls for stoning adulterers (Leviticus 20:10; stoning was the usual form of capital punishment—Numbers 15:35). If he favors severity, he will be challenging the Roman government, which reserves for itself the authority to impose capital punishment.

Obviously, the questioners are not sincerely seeking the truth. Worse, they are using the woman as a pawn in their game. Because they show contempt for human life—and wrap their corrupt set of values in religious packaging—Jesus does not give them the courtesy of a response. He acts as though they are not there—a gesture of rejection that speaks louder than words. Even when the questioners persist, Jesus refuses to answer their question. He does, however, give them a reply that makes it impossible for them to continue with the execution: if they proceed, they will expose themselves to ridicule for claiming to be sinless.

Soon the woman is left alone with Jesus. After the woman's close brush with death, Jesus apparently does not feel that she needs a lecture on the evils of adultery. He lets her go with a simple warning.

Luke 23:32–43. As Jesus hangs dying between two criminals, perhaps some of those who mock him are thinking, "He wanted to be with sinners. Well, now he's getting what he wanted!" Indeed, Jesus *is* getting what he wanted—not that he wanted to die, but he does want to be among sinners. Crucifixion gives him the opportunity to talk with a dying man. Their conversation will determine the man's condition for eternity. Jesus has pursued his ministry of personal presence to sinners all the way from Levi's dining room in Galilee to a cross at Golgotha.

Jesus' reconciliation of a dying criminal to God symbolizes the larger effect of his death. By giving his life on the cross, Jesus opens the way for all sinful men and women to be reconciled to God (Luke 24:46–47).

Reflections. Jesus never treats sin lightly. He speaks of Levi and his toll-collector friends as sick people who need a doctor. He acknowledges that the woman at Simon's dinner has been a great sinner, for his parable points to her as someone who has experienced great forgiveness, which only a great sinner can receive. His instruction to the woman caught in adultery is brief but clear: "Do not sin again" (John 8:11). He accepts as true the criminal's self-evaluation—"we are getting what we deserve" (Luke 23:41). But Jesus does not fixate on people's sins. He is mainly concerned with extending God's forgiveness. He focuses on inviting men and women to be his disciples, on giving them a second chance, on assuring them that God's forgiveness is real, on leading them into paradise.

Significantly, the precise moment of repentance in the lives of those with whom Jesus interacts is often obscure. When does Levi repent: somewhere along the road as he follows Jesus? When does the woman at Simon's banquet repent: in a conversation with Jesus not recorded in the Gospels? What about the woman dragged before Jesus in the temple? It is hard to say. Jesus does not deal with people's confession of sin in public. Except at the cross, where it is impossible to escape the public gaze, he seems to treat reconciliation as a private matter. In their accounts, the Gospel writers have shown a similar discretion.

Questions for Reflection and Discussion

45 minutes
Choose questions according to your interest and time.

1 How do you picture Jesus relating to Levi and the other guests at Levi's dinner party: Did he preach? Did he make small talk? Did he have a good time? What do you base your picture on?

2 Try looking at Jesus' call of Levi from the viewpoint of his earlier disciples. Perhaps Peter, James, and John have been victims of Levi's toll collecting in the past, when they were transporting their catches of fish to market. Now Jesus has added Levi to the group of disciples. How do you think they will respond? How will Levi respond?

3 Who are the toll collectors of today? What does Jesus' example suggest about how people should relate to them?

4 What do you think the woman's accusers expected Jesus to say (John 8:4–5)? Can you support your view from other things they might have known about Jesus' views?

5 What kinds of encouragement do people receive in today's society to pay attention to other people's sins and ignore their own?

6 How is it possible to reject sin but not the sinner? Describe a situation in which you saw it happen—or experienced it yourself.

7 For personal reflection: Reread Jesus' statement in Luke 5:31–32. What do Jesus' words mean for your relationship with him?

8 **Focus question:** What difficulties might a person encounter who attempted to imitate Jesus' way of relating to people in this week's readings? How could a person grow in imitating him? What specific step could you take this coming week in imitation of Jesus?

Prayer to Close

10 minutes
Use this approach—or create your own!

◆ Let someone read Matthew 7:1–5 aloud. Pause for silent reflection. Then pray together this prayer by St. Ephrem. Close with an Our Father.

My Lord and King, grant me the ability to see my own sins and not to judge my brother or sister, for you are blessed forever and ever. Amen.

A Living Tradition

Jesus Merciful and True

*This section is a supplement for individual reading.
From St. Augustine's commentary on John 8.*

When everyone else had gone and the woman was left alone, Jesus looked up at her. She became more frightened, I think, when she heard the Lord say, "Let anyone among you who is without sin be the first to throw a stone at her" (John 8:7). For they, turning their attention to themselves and acknowledging their sin by leaving, had left the sinful woman with him who was without sin. And because she had heard him say, "Let anyone among you who is without sin be the first to throw a stone at her," she expected to be punished by him in whom no sin could be found. But he who had driven away her accusers with a word of justice, looking at her with gentleness asked her, "Has no one condemned you?" (8:10). She answered, "No one, sir" (8:11). And said, "Neither do I condemn you" (8:11).

Lord, what is this? Are you promoting sin? Obviously not! Consider what follows: "Go your way, and from now on do not sin again" (8:11). So the Lord *does* condemn—but sin, not the sinner. If he had become a promoter of sin, he would have said, "Neither do I condemn you. Go, and live as you wish and be confident that I will save you. For no matter how much you sin, I will save you from any punishment, even from the torments of hell." But that is not what he said.

Therefore, let those who take pleasure in the Lord's gentleness think about this and fear his truth. . . . The Lord is gentle, the Lord is patient, the Lord is merciful; but the Lord is also just and true. He delays judgment to give you the opportunity to change your ways; you, however, like the delay but dislike the change.

Were you bad yesterday? Today be good. Did you carry out evil today? Well, change tomorrow. You are always expecting a lot of mercy from God; you even promise it to yourself—as though he who promised you forgiveness if you repent also promised to extend your opportunity for repenting. How do you know what tomorrow may bring? You are right to think, "When I change, God will forgive all my sins.". . . But from which prophet can you quote to me a promise that God will give you a long life?

. . . TO PEOPLE HE MET ALONG THE WAY

Questions to Begin

10 minutes
Use a question or two to get warmed up for the reading.

1 What possession do you find hard to share?

2 If you could have anyone in the world come to your home for dinner, who would it be?

We read Scripture and we meditate so that correct decisions are born and the consoling strength of the Spirit might help us put them into practice.

Cardinal Carlo Maria Martini, *The Joy of the Gospel*

Opening the Bible

*10 minutes
Read the passage aloud. Let individuals take turns reading
paragraphs.*

The Background

Our readings this week are a bit of a grab bag. The main thing the
people in these episodes have in common is—they're different.
Jesus was constantly moving around and meeting people as he
went. He ran into all kinds of people, with all sorts of needs,
requests, and questions. Our readings here give us the chance to
observe Jesus dealing with different people in different situations.
What common features can you observe in the way that Jesus
relates to these varied people? We, too, are always meeting people
along the way in our own lives. What does Jesus' example suggest
about how we might relate to them?

The Reading: Luke 12:13–21; Mark 10:13–16;
Luke 19:1–10; 23:27–31

A Man in the Crowd

Luke 12:13 Someone in the crowd said to him, "Teacher, tell my brother
to divide the family inheritance with me." 14 But he said to him,
"Friend, who set me to be a judge or arbitrator over you?"

15 And he said to them, "Take care! Be on your guard against
all kinds of greed; for one's life does not consist in the abundance of
possessions."

16 Then he told them a parable: "The land of a rich man
produced abundantly. 17 And he thought to himself, 'What should I
do, for I have no place to store my crops?' 18 Then he said, 'I will do
this: I will pull down my barns and build larger ones, and there I will
store all my grain and my goods. 19 And I will say to my soul, 'Soul,
you have ample goods laid up for many years; relax, eat, drink, be
merry.' 20 But God said to him, 'You fool! This very night your life is
being demanded of you. And the things you have prepared, whose

will they be?' 21 So it is with those who store up treasures for themselves but are not rich toward God."

Parents and Children

Mark 10:13 People were bringing little children to him in order that he might touch them; and the disciples spoke sternly to them. 14 But when Jesus saw this, he was indignant and said to them, "Let the little children come to me; do not stop them; for it is to such as these that the kingdom of God belongs. 15 Truly I tell you, whoever does not receive the kingdom of God as a little child will never enter it." 16 And he took them up in his arms, laid his hands on them, and blessed them.

Another Toll Collector

Luke 19:1 He entered Jericho and was passing through it. 2 A man was there named Zacchaeus; he was a chief tax collector and was rich. 3 He was trying to see who Jesus was, but on account of the crowd he could not, because he was short in stature. 4 So he ran ahead and climbed a sycamore tree to see him, because he was going to pass that way. 5 When Jesus came to the place, he looked up and said to him, "Zacchaeus, hurry and come down; for I must stay at your house today." 6 So he hurried down and was happy to welcome him.

7 All who saw it began to grumble and said, "He has gone to be the guest of one who is a sinner."

8 Zacchaeus stood there and said to the Lord, "Look, half of my possessions, Lord, I will give to the poor; and if I have defrauded anyone of anything, I will pay back four times as much."

9 Then Jesus said to him, "Today salvation has come to this house, because he too is a son of Abraham. 10 For the Son of Man came to seek out and to save the lost."

Grief-stricken Women

Luke 23:27 A great number of the people followed him, and among them were women who were beating their breasts and wailing for him. 28 But Jesus turned to them and said, "Daughters of Jerusalem, do not weep for me, but weep for yourselves and for your children. [29] For the days are surely coming when they will say, 'Blessed are the barren, and the wombs that never bore, and the breasts that never nursed.' [30] Then they will begin to say to the mountains, 'Fall on us'; and to the hills, 'Cover us.' [31] For if they do this when the wood is green, what will happen when it is dry?"

First Impression

5 minutes
Briefly mention a question you have about the reading or one thing in it that surprised, impressed, delighted, or challenged you. No discussion! Just listen to one another's reactions.

Exploring the Theme

If participants have not read this section already, read it aloud.
Otherwise go on to "Questions for Reflection and Discussion."

Luke 12:13–21. Here's the situation: two brothers have inherited joint ownership of the family farmland; one of them wants to divide it, the other does not. A great deal may be at stake. If it is the older brother who does not want to divide the land, he may be trying to force his younger brother out. This would send the dispossessed brother into economic free fall.

In first-century Palestine, religious leaders are sometimes asked to adjudicate inheritance disputes, so the man's appeal to Jesus is not surprising. What's surprising is that Jesus declines. It is an honor to act as arbitrator. But the matter lies outside Jesus' mission. In earlier readings we observed how readily Jesus makes himself available to people who seek him out. Here we see the other side of the coin: he refuses to get involved in matters he regards as none of his business.

Instead, Jesus uses the man's request as a springboard for a brief sermon. His parable is a warning against "greed." The Greek word used here means "being insatiable." Jesus does not explain what is wrong with the plans of the wealthy farmer in the parable, but he doesn't need to. His listeners know. If this farmer has brought in a good harvest, probably neighboring farmers have too. Consequently a lot of grain will be coming to market, and the price will fall. So this farmer decides to withhold his grain from the market to force the price up. Although the low price is bad for the sellers, it is, of course, good for the buyers. Low grain prices are especially good for poor people, for whom fluctuations in the price of grain can be a matter of life and death. If the farmer in the parable succeeds in forcing up the price of grain, some of his poor neighbors will go hungry.

The farmer's behavior drew a chorus of criticisms from bishops in the early Church. St. Cyril of Alexandria (Egypt, fourth–fifth centuries) remarked: "He does not sympathize with suffering. It gives him no pain nor awakens his pity." St. Augustine (same period, in present-day Algeria), wrote: "He was planning to fill his soul with excessive and unnecessary feasting and was proudly disregarding all those empty bellies of the poor. He did not realize that the bellies of the poor were much safer storerooms than his barns. What he was stowing away in those barns was perhaps even then being stolen away by thieves. But if he stowed it away in the bellies of the poor, it would of course be digested on earth, but in heaven it would be kept all the more safely."

The farmer's plan to tear down his existing barns and replace them, rather than extend his existing barns, indicates that he intends to keep as much of his land in production as possible—and is expecting further bumper crops. Thus he acts as though he is in control of future harvests. "Still more irrational," Cyril observes, "he settles for himself the length of his life, as if he would reap this also from the ground" (12:18–19). The farmer regards his store of grain as his own. But really, not even his life is his. His life is on loan to him from God, and he has no way of knowing when the loan will come due.

The farmer enters eternity without his grain—or anything else. "The things that we cannot take with us are not ours," remarks St. Ambrose (Italy, fourth century). "Virtue is the only companion of the dead. Compassion alone follows us." The farmer faces eternal life without heavenly treasure. The implication is very grim.

The man who asked Jesus to settle the dispute with his brother goes home with his conflict unresolved. He may be facing impoverishment. But Jesus has given him something even more important to consider.

Mark 10:13–16. The disciples see themselves as guardians of Jesus' public standing. They think that his being mobbed by little children will detract from his prestige as a teacher. Jesus objects. The disciples are treating children as less important than adults, but, Jesus points out, children provide an image of the kind of people that adults must become if they are to enter God's kingdom—people who recognize their helplessness and trust their heavenly Father to care for them. Besides, Jesus likes children. The scene is often noted for Jesus' affection for the children. It is equally notable for Jesus' anger toward his disciples. He was not at all pleased by their evaluating people's importance according to a worldly scale of values.

Luke 19:1–10. Jesus' satisfaction with Zacchaeus is surprising in light of his conversation with the rich man along the road (Luke 18:18–25; we read Mark's version in Week 2). Jesus told that earlier rich man to distribute *all* his wealth to the poor. Here Jesus announces, "Today salvation has come to this house," even though Zacchaeus keeps half his wealth. Apparently the requirement Jesus set for the first wealthy man was geared to the man's particular spiritual condition: money was an idol for him, and the only thing to do with an idol is to smash it. Perhaps money does not have such a hold on Zacchaeus. Jesus deals with each person individually. The two episodes have a common feature, however: both show Jesus as someone who disapproves of loving money and approves of generosity to those in need.

Is Zacchaeus expressing repentance? Perhaps not. In the Greek text of verse 8, he says, "I give" and "I pay" (NRSV translates this as "I will give . . . I will pay"). Zacchaeus may be describing what he is already doing rather than announcing what he is going to do. In the opinion of New Testament scholar Joseph Fitzmyer, S.J., Jesus announces salvation to Zacchaeus's house not because Zacchaeus is now deciding to turn from dishonest, moneygrubbing ways but because he has been handling his material resources honestly and charitably. Jesus knows that, contrary to public opinion, Zacchaeus is innocent—a true "son of Abraham"—despite the negative assumption that people make about him because of his job. If Father Fitzmyer is right, Zacchaeus is like the woman who barged in on Simon's dinner. Both are considered great sinners by the people around them. But, unbeknownst to other people, they have become devoted to God.

By declaring that Zacchaeus has a relationship with God, Jesus refutes the criticism that has cut Zacchaeus off from the community. Part of Jesus' ministry consists in setting individuals free from the low esteem in which others hold them—as we saw him doing with the woman at Simon's house. By Jesus' declaration, Zacchaeus is rehabilitated as a member of the community.

Jesus seems to take it for granted that people are not necessarily as society perceives them. A bunch of scruffy children may be model citizens of God's kingdom. A toll collector may be an example for how to handle one's money.

Luke 23:27–31. These women are almost the last people Jesus meets on his journey through earthly life. He passes them in the street as he staggers to the place of execution. The women weep at the sight of his tortured body and the thought of the agonizing death he is about to undergo. But Jesus tells them to save their tears for suffering yet to come. He foresees the catastrophe that will befall Jerusalem when Roman armies crush a Jewish revolt a generation or so after his death, in AD 70. He has already wept at the thought of it (Luke 19:41–44). As he goes to his death, this looming suffering of the people of Jerusalem seems more important to him than his own.

Reflections. Jesus must have seemed unpredictable to his disciples. (Mary and Joseph could have warned them!) He declines the honor of acting as an arbitrator. He becomes incensed at his disciples for defending his dignity from a crowd of children. For his luncheon venue he chooses the home of a man the neighbors regard as a scoundrel. He rejects the condolences of people who are filled with sorrow at his sufferings. Perhaps our readings help us understand why some people thought he was crazy (Mark 3:21).

The consistent element in Jesus' unconventional behavior is his concern for other people. He does not mind being mobbed by children, because it gives him the opportunity to bless them. He risks social disapproval in order to draw a despised man back into the community. Faced with a choice between gaining people's esteem and being with those he feels called to serve, Jesus accepts disapproval every time. His attitude is that if exercising his ministry of teaching, healing, and rehabilitating people reduces his public standing, well, so be it. This is humility in action.

Questions for Reflection and Discussion

45 minutes
Choose questions according to your interest and time.

1 In Luke 12:13–15, does Jesus accuse the man who requests arbitration of having a bad attitude toward money?

2 Jesus knows Zacchaeus before Zacchaeus knows Jesus (Luke 19:5). How?

3 When have you discovered that someone was different—in a good way—from your original impression of them? How has this experience affected you?

4 When has concern for other people's opinion held you back from doing something that might have been helpful to someone else? If you could go back to the situation, what would you do differently?

5 When have you seen someone look beyond their own difficulties and suffering to care for someone else? How can one grow in being that kind of person?

6 For personal reflection: In what ways is your sense of a person's importance affected by their money or power, their celebrity status or good looks—or lack of them? How is Jesus' view of a person affected by these qualities? How could you grow in looking at people the way Jesus does?

7 **Focus question:** Whose efforts to do good often go unnoticed or unthanked in your family? your parish? your work situation? Who tends to be treated as less important, less deserving of attention? What could you do to give thanks or recognition to these people?

Prayer to Close

10 minutes
Use this approach—or create your own!

◆ Begin together with an Our Father. Then take a couple of minutes to remember people you have met along the way during the last week. Pray the following prayer together. Close with a Hail Mary and a Glory Be.

Loving God, we pray for all those who have come into our lives, even briefly, this last week, and for all those who will come our way in this coming week. Help us to value each person as you do. Help us to be available to all those you put into our care in any way. Help us to see where you wish us to get involved—and where you do not wish us to get involved. Free us from greed and self-seeking. Enable us to look beyond our own sorrows and needs to feel compassion for the people around us.

Saints in the Making

Seeing Christ in All

This section is a supplement for individual reading.

Caryll Houselander was an unusual person. A British artist, she made her living as a wood carver of religious objects and as a spiritual writer. She lived in a tiny London apartment, maintained a wide and varied network of friends, wrote late at night in her bathroom, and loved her cat so deeply that his death was one of the saddest moments of her life (he had lived with her for twenty years). Houselander was convinced that God calls each person to a "personal apostolate." One of the most striking features of her apostolate was that, like Jesus, she dealt with each person individually.

During the Depression and World War II (Houselander lived from 1901 to 1954), lots of people in London needed material help but would be offended by any offer of charity. So Houselander organized a secret club called the Loaves and the Fishes. The group secretly solicited donations, then cleverly got the funds to needy people in devious ways. They paid a nurse to visit a mother with a sick baby. They helped a Russian refugee countess by paying her to pose while they painted her (several in the club were artists). They invented an imaginary competition in which a poor schoolteacher "won" a sum of money that allowed her to have urgent dental work performed. At one point, there were a hundred "fishes," as they called themselves, discretely locating contributors and delivering "loaves" to recipients who often had no idea what was going on.

A prominent psychologist asked Houselander to spend time with some emotionally disturbed boys in his care. She worked with them one-on-one using drawing and music. Houselander had a knack for penetrating each child's inner world. Of one boy she wrote, he "has a mind like a beautiful valley almost hidden by a dark and shadowing twilight. In that twilight one hears the sound of tears and yet finds rare and isolated flowers growing, and these flowers have a positively sparkling brilliance."

Houselander was motivated by an all-embracing vision of Christ. "We must begin by making acts of faith in the presence of Christ in our own souls," she wrote—and then go on to seek in him the soul of each person we encounter.

. . . TO THOSE WHO REJECTED HIM

Questions to Begin

10 minutes
Use a question or two to get warmed up for the reading.

1 Describe a time when you had trouble finding a place to eat or lodge when you were away from home. How did things turn out?

2 In the home where you grew up, did people consider cleanliness near to godliness? How near?

We cannot understand the Scriptures with a sophisticated mind and a self-complacent attitude. We must be ready to be recreated by God's Word.

Damasus Winzen, O.S.B., *Pathways in Scripture*

Opening the Bible

10 minutes
Read the passage aloud. Let individuals take turns reading
paragraphs.

The Background

Jesus faced rejection in many forms. On at least one occasion
(our first reading) people refused him hospitality. Religious leaders
called Pharisees (our second reading) opposed him because he
disagreed with their traditions for applying the Mosaic law to daily
life. The authorities in charge of the temple in Jerusalem (our third
reading) treated Jesus as a threat to the political arrangement
they enjoyed with the Romans. Eventually they seized him and
turned him over to the Roman governor with a charge calculated
to bring his execution. In our fourth reading, we listen to Jesus
speaking with this governor. Jesus responded in various ways to
these different situations. Our fifth reading brings us to the heart
of all Jesus' responses to rejection.

The Reading: Luke 9:51–56; 11:37–44; Mark 11:27–33; John 18:33–19:12; Luke 23:32–34

Villagers Who Refused Him Hospitality

Luke 9:51 When the days drew near for him to be taken up, he set his
face to go to Jerusalem. 52 And he sent messengers ahead of him. On
their way they entered a village of the Samaritans to make ready for
him; 53 but they did not receive him, because his face was set toward
Jerusalem. 54 When his disciples James and John saw it, they said,
"Lord, do you want us to command fire to come down from heaven
and consume them?" 55 But he turned and rebuked them. 56 Then
they went on to another village.

A Man Who Criticized His Behavior

Luke 11:37 While he was speaking, a Pharisee invited him to dine with
him; so he went in and took his place at the table. 38 The Pharisee was
amazed to see that he did not first wash before dinner. 39 Then the Lord
said to him, "Now you Pharisees clean the outside of the cup and of
the dish, but inside you are full of greed and wickedness. 40 You fools!
Did not the one who made the outside make the inside also? 41 So
give for alms those things that are within; and see, everything will be
clean for you.

42 "But woe to you Pharisees! For you tithe mint and rue and herbs of all kinds, and neglect justice and the love of God; it is these you ought to have practiced, without neglecting the others. 43 Woe to you Pharisees! For you love to have the seat of honor in the synagogues and to be greeted with respect in the marketplaces. 44 Woe to you! For you are like unmarked graves, and people walk over them without realizing it."

Religious Experts Who Laid Traps for Him

Mark 11:27 Again they came to Jerusalem. As he was walking in the temple, the chief priests, the scribes, and the elders came to him 28 and said, "By what authority are you doing these things? Who gave you this authority to do them?" 29 Jesus said to them, "I will ask you one question; answer me, and I will tell you by what authority I do these things. 30 Did the baptism of John come from heaven, or was it of human origin? Answer me." 31 They argued with one another, "If we say, 'From heaven,' he will say, 'Why then did you not believe him?' 32 But shall we say, 'Of human origin'?"—they were afraid of the crowd, for all regarded John as truly a prophet. 33 So they answered Jesus, "We do not know." And Jesus said to them, "Neither will I tell you by what authority I am doing these things."

The Governor Who Condemned Him

John 18:33 Then Pilate entered the headquarters again, summoned Jesus, and asked him, "Are you the King of the Jews?" 34 Jesus answered, "Do you ask this on your own, or did others tell you about me?" 35 Pilate replied, "I am not a Jew, am I? Your own nation and the chief priests have handed you over to me. What have you done?" 36 Jesus answered, "My kingdom is not from this world. If my kingdom were from this world, my followers would be fighting to keep me from being handed over to the Jews. But as it is, my kingdom is not from here." 37 Pilate asked him, "So you are a king?"

Jesus answered, "You say that I am a king. For this I was born, and for this I came into the world, to testify to the truth. Everyone who belongs to the truth listens to my voice." 38 Pilate asked him, "What is truth?"

After he had said this, he went out to the Jews again and told them, "I find no case against him. 39 But you have a custom that I release someone for you at the Passover. Do you want me to release

for you the King of the Jews?" 40 They shouted in reply, "Not this
man, but Barabbas!" Now Barabbas was a bandit.

19:1 Then Pilate took Jesus and had him flogged. 2 And the
soldiers wove a crown of thorns and put it on his head, and they
dressed him in a purple robe. 3 They kept coming up to him, saying,
"Hail, King of the Jews!" and striking him on the face. 4 Pilate went
out again and said to them, "Look, I am bringing him out to you to
let you know that I find no case against him." 5 So Jesus came out,
wearing the crown of thorns and the purple robe. Pilate said to them,
"Here is the man!" 6 When the chief priests and the police saw him,
they shouted, "Crucify him! Crucify him!" Pilate said to them, "Take
him yourselves and crucify him; I find no case against him." 7 The
Jews answered him, "We have a law, and according to that law he
ought to die because he has claimed to be the Son of God."

8 Now when Pilate heard this, he was more afraid than ever.
9 He entered his headquarters again and asked Jesus, "Where are you
from?" But Jesus gave him no answer. 10 Pilate therefore said to him,
"Do you refuse to speak to me? Do you not know that I have power
to release you, and power to crucify you?" 11 Jesus answered him,
"You would have no power over me unless it had been given you
from above; therefore the one who handed me over to you is guilty
of a greater sin." 12 From then on Pilate tried to release him.

All Who Were Responsible for His Death

Luke 23:32 Two others also, who were criminals, were led away to be
put to death with him. 33 When they came to the place that is called
The Skull, they crucified Jesus there with the criminals, one on his
right and one on his left. 34 Then Jesus said, "Father, forgive them; for
they do not know what they are doing."

First Impression

5 minutes
*Briefly mention a question you have about the reading or one
thing in it that surprised, impressed, delighted, or challenged you.
No discussion! Just listen to one another's reactions.*

Exploring the Theme

If participants have not read this section already, read it aloud.
Otherwise go on to "Questions for Reflection and Discussion."

Luke 9:51–56. The Samaritans once had a temple of their own, near the present-day Palestinian city of Nablus, but a Jewish army destroyed it. After that, understandably, Samaritans felt cool toward Jews traveling through Samaria on the way to their Jewish temple in Jerusalem. So there is probably nothing personal in these villagers' refusal to offer hospitality to Jesus. They close their doors on Jesus not because of anything he has said or done but simply because he is Jewish.

The Old Testament prophet Elijah had called down heavenly fire on his opponents (2 Kings 1:9–12). Jesus' disciples would be happy to administer the same treatment to the unfriendly Samaritans. Like John the Baptist, the disciples expect Jesus to carry out an Elijah-type ministry of judgment (compare Luke 7:18–23—Week 2). But Jesus disappoints them.

Luke 11:37–44. Once again, Jesus is invited to dine at a Pharisee's home (recall Luke 7:36–50—Week 3). Perhaps this Pharisee, like Simon, is open to Jesus but has some doubts about him. If so, his doubts are soon confirmed. In the Pharisee's view, ceremonial hand washing (not required by the law of Moses) is a mark of submission to God's law; it distinguishes those who are serious about obeying God from those who aren't. Jesus is familiar with the Pharisee's views, so his failure to practice the ritual here is a calculated challenge to his host.

If there had been a first-century Miss Manners, she would have insisted that banquets are not the place for personal criticisms. Jesus, however, has already shown that niceness is not his highest social value (Luke 7:44–47). Sensing his host's critical thoughts, Jesus accuses him of hypocrisy—of trying to impress people with religious behavior while hiding a selfish agenda.

Jesus must have a good reason for embarrassing his host this way. In fact, an important issue is at stake: what is the right way to show faithfulness to God? In Jesus' view, the Pharisees are too concerned about avoiding ceremonial impurity and not concerned enough about avoiding a worse kind of impurity—impurity of the heart, which consists of lack of concern for other peoples' needs. Jesus reminds his host that God is as concerned about a person's heart as he is about a person's hands. Intentions, as well as actions, are important in God's eyes.

Jesus' words to his host are negative. Yet he points his host toward the way out of his spiritual dead end: his host should give away what he loves (11:41); he should cleanse his heart of greed by giving his money to the needy. This is basically the same advice Jesus gave to the rich man (Mark 10:21—Week 2). Jesus' "woe to you" statements are not condemnations but warnings: "Dear Pharisee, watch out! You will end up very unhappy if you continue on your present course of action."

Mark 11:27–33. The men who question Jesus do not want to know the answer to their question. They are already convinced that Jesus lacks divine authorization. They simply want him to put his claim to divine authorization into words so that they will have a damning quotation to use against him.

Earlier, Jesus embarrassed a Pharisee who was critical of his behavior. Now he traps his opponents into embarrassing themselves. His question draws from them a reply that any observer can recognize as false. At this time, John the Baptist is big news (Mark 1:4–5; Luke 3:15). No one would believe that these lofty religious leaders, who are supposed to evaluate alleged prophets, do not have an opinion on whether John was sent by God.

Jesus is a humble man—he has come to serve, even to lay down his life in service to others (Mark 10:45)—but he has not come to be used. He is willing to endure scorn and humiliation if it serves a good purpose, but he refuses to cooperate with people who want to manipulate him.

John 18:33–19:12. In Jerusalem, a council of religious leaders and wealthy landowners governs the temple and city under the Romans' direction. This council is not an elected body; it does not represent the views of most Jews in Palestine (see Matthew 26:3–5). The high priest, who heads the council, is handpicked by the Romans for his usefulness in maintaining their rule. Later Jewish writings reflect the anger that many Jews of the time felt about the dishonesty and ruthlessness of some of these council members.

The council has devised a plan for getting rid of Jesus. Possibly they have coordinated their actions with Pilate ahead of time. They will accuse Jesus of claiming to be the king of the Jews, in effect, a rebel leader. Pilate will then execute Jesus in the most painful and humiliating way available—by crucifixion. But when the council seizes Jesus and turns him over to Pilate, Pilate proves to be uncooperative. In fact, he uses the situation to embarrass the council members by reminding them of the limits of their authority (18:31) and making fun of them (18:39).

Caught between the council's hatred and Pilate's indifference, Jesus is powerless, in purely human terms. Yet he calmly insists on his identity as king of God's people. No verbal or physical abuse can shake his confidence in who he is in God's eyes. Jesus knows that he is bringing God's kingdom of forgiveness, grace, love, and eternal life into the world (18:37). Amid accusations and torture, Jesus continues to bear witness to this truth, even to those who are sending him to his death.

Jesus' certitude about himself and his role in God's plans emerges with particular clarity in his conversations with Pilate. As Pilate interrogates Jesus, Jesus interrogates Pilate. He declares the truth to Pilate and insists that Pilate take a position for it or against it. When Pilate repeats the charge of kingship, Jesus responds, in effect, "I wouldn't have publicly proclaimed my kingship. But since you ask about it, yes, I am king. And where do *you* stand with regard to my rule?" (see 18:37). Jesus the prisoner puts Pilate the judge on trial.

His final conversation with Pilate is Jesus' last chance to avoid the cross. But rather than pleading for his life, Jesus uses the opportunity to confront Pilate with the issue of his account-ability (19:11). Jesus' words constitute a warning to Pilate that by condemning Jesus he will bring judgment on himself.

Luke 23:32–34. In the agony of crucifixion, Jesus pleads with God to forgive all those who have had a hand in his suffering, from the temple council to the execution squad. Jesus has enemies, in the sense that there are people who have sought to harm him. In another sense, however, Jesus has no enemies, for he does not seek to harm anyone—not even those who have brought about his death.

Reflections. Our readings expose the complexity of Jesus' character. From other Gospel episodes, such as his clearing merchants out of the temple, we know that he was certainly capable of anger (John 2:13–17). Yet here we see how mild he could be toward those who opposed him. Encountering insult and inconvenience in Samaria, he simply moved on. He did not, however, always avoid conflict. At times, he disregarded social niceties and dragged hidden conflicts into the open. Thinking that his dinner host needed a sharp warning, Jesus gave it to him straight.

Kindhearted, fond of children, and sensitive to people's needs, Jesus was nonetheless realistic about people. He knew what his questioners in the temple were up to (Mark 11:27–33). He refused to let himself be bullied by scheming questioners or even by the Roman governor who held his life in his hands. In the face of overwhelming power, Jesus refused to be intimidated. He remained committed to his mission no matter how much he was made to suffer. In fact, even in his suffering he looked beyond himself to the welfare of those who tormented him. He was as concerned about the consequences of Pilate's decision for Pilate as about the consequences for himself.

At Golgotha, Jesus revealed his longing for all people to experience reconciliation with God. Many of his statements in the Gospels reflect his conviction that sins have painful consequences. But his prayer—"Father, forgive them; for they do not know what they are doing" (Luke 23:34)—reveals that he had no desire for anyone to suffer the consequences of sin. Indeed, enabling us to avoid those consequences was the reason he went to the cross.

Questions for Reflection and Discussion

45 minutes
Choose questions according to your interest and time.

1 Jesus had instructed his disciples in how to relate to people who treated them badly (Luke 6:27–36). So why would James and John make their suggestion in Luke 9:54?

2 Why does Jesus use harsh language in speaking to the Pharisee who invites him to dinner (Luke 11:40, 44)?

3 In Mark 11:27–33, what answer would Jesus' questioners like to hear from him?

4 Jesus' question to the religious leaders cleverly leads them to show their insincerity. Is it possible to imitate Jesus' quick-wittedness?

5 What does the scene of Jesus' scourging (John 19:1–3) contribute to the total picture of Jesus in the reading from John's Gospel?

6 What could be learned from Jesus' behavior in these readings about when conflict should be avoided and when it should be brought into the open?

7   What aspect of Jesus' behavior in these readings might be a pointer for how you could deal with some situation in your life?

8   For personal reflection: What aspect of Jesus' behavior in these readings would you find hardest to imitate? Why? How could you become more like him?

9   **Focus question:** Choose one of this week's readings and consider how Jesus relates to the people in it. Identify a present-day situation where a person might be able to imitate Jesus. What difference could imitating him make for people in this situation? What might be the cost for the person trying to follow Jesus' example? When have you seen someone handle a situation the way Jesus did?

Prayer to Close

10 minutes
Use this approach—or create your own!

◆ Let one person read Luke 6:27–36 aloud. Pause for silent reflection. Allow time for anyone who wishes to offer a brief prayer. Then pray together this Byzantine Christian prayer.

Lord Jesus Christ, in your great mercy you prayed for the forgiveness of those who crucified you, and you taught us to love our enemies and to pray for those who persecute us. Lord, I pray that you would forgive those who treat me unjustly and speak against me. Bless them and guide them according to your will. Take away any bitterness I may have in my heart against them. Lord, may your forgiveness, goodness, and love be revealed in all of us, to your praise and glory. Amen.

Saints in the Making

A Father's Grief

This section is a supplement for individual reading.

Twenty-year-old Tariq Khamisa was delivering pizzas in San Diego on a Saturday night in January 1995. At his last stop, four youths demanded his pizzas. When he refused, an eighteen-year-old member of the group handed a gun to a fourteen-year-old eighth-grader named Tony Hicks and told him to shoot Khamisa. Hicks fired a single bullet into Tariq's heart.

Tariq's death devastated his family. "I felt like a nuclear bomb detonated inside of me," Tariq's father, Azim Khamisa said. But when a friend told Khamisa he hoped the killer would fry in hell, Khamisa replied, "I don't see it that way. There were victims on both ends of the gun." Trying to deal with his pain, Khamisa, a Muslim in the Isma'ili tradition, turned to the Qur'an. He was especially struck by a line in the Qur'an which says that righteousness is giving of one's resources to kinfolk, orphans, the needy, and travelers out of love for God (Qur'an 2:177). Khamisa reflected on the Muslim concept of human brotherhood. Afterward, he consulted a spiritual counselor in his religious tradition. "He encouraged me to do good deeds," Khamisa says, "which would transfer to my son's soul and help speed his journey."

"I felt my country should do more for its children," Khamisa says. "Its children are not born gangsters. In fact, they have in them the potential to be heroes." Khamisa met Tony Hicks's grandfather and guardian, Ples Felix, and let him know that he felt no bitterness toward his family. Khamisa and Felix, who was raised as a Baptist, decided to take action. They formed an association, called the Violence Impact Forum, which uses multimedia presentations, including their own story, to educate children in schools about gangs and violence.

Khamisa has reduced the time he spends on his investment banking business in order to carry out this work, which he feels is a mission from God. "I will mourn Tariq's death for the rest of my life," he says. "Now, however, grief has been transformed into a powerful commitment to change. Change is urgently needed in a society where children kill children."

Tony Hicks was the first juvenile tried for murder as an adult in California. He is serving a sentence of twenty-five years to life for killing Tariq Khamisa.

. . . TO HIS FRIENDS

Questions to Begin

10 minutes
Use a question or two to get warmed up for the reading.

1 Which of your friends have you known the longest?

2 Who is literally your oldest friend?

It is absolutely impossible that anyone should understand what he hears of the word of God if he is not completely honest before God and has [not] determined to surrender his life, his responsibilities, his interests, his money, his future, and his honor, and lay them at God's feet.

Abbot Matta El-Meskeen, *How to Read the Bible*

Opening the Bible

10 minutes
Read the passage aloud. Let individuals take turns reading paragraphs.

The Background

Jesus had many friends, including all his disciples (John 15:14). But the Gospels tell us about three friends in particular. Here we read the three Gospel incidents in which they appear.

The Reading: Selections from Luke 10:38–42; John 11:1–45; 12:1–8

Dinner with Friends

Luke 10:38 Now as they went on their way, he entered a certain village, where a woman named Martha welcomed him into her home. 39 She had a sister named Mary, who sat at the Lord's feet and listened to what he was saying. 40 But Martha was distracted by her many tasks; so she came to him and asked, "Lord, do you not care that my sister has left me to do all the work by myself? Tell her then to help me."

41 But the Lord answered her, "Martha, Martha, you are worried and distracted by many things; 42 there is need of only one thing. Mary has chosen the better part, which will not be taken away from her."

Jesus' Greatest Sign

John 11:1 Now a certain man was ill, Lazarus of Bethany, the village of Mary and her sister Martha. 2 Mary was the one who anointed the Lord with perfume and wiped his feet with her hair; her brother Lazarus was ill. 3 So the sisters sent a message to Jesus, "Lord, he whom you love is ill."

4 But when Jesus heard it, he said, "This illness does not lead to death; rather it is for God's glory, so that the Son of God may be glorified through it." 5 Accordingly, though Jesus loved Martha and her sister and Lazarus, 6 after having heard that Lazarus was ill, he stayed two days longer in the place where he was.

7 Then after this he said to the disciples, "Let us go to Judea again." 8 The disciples said to him, "Rabbi, the Jews were just now trying to stone you, and are you going there again?" 9 Jesus answered,

"Are there not twelve hours of daylight? Those who walk during the day do not stumble, because they see the light of this world. 10 But those who walk at night stumble, because the light is not in them." 11 After saying this, he told them, "Our friend Lazarus has fallen asleep, but I am going there to awaken him." 12 The disciples said to him, "Lord, if he has fallen asleep, he will be all right." 13 Jesus, however, had been speaking about his death, but they thought that he was referring merely to sleep. 14 Then Jesus told them plainly, "Lazarus is dead. 15 For your sake I am glad I was not there, so that you may believe. But let us go to him." . . .

17 When Jesus arrived, he found that Lazarus had already been in the tomb four days. 18 Now Bethany was near Jerusalem, some two miles away, 19 and many of the Jews had come to Martha and Mary to console them about their brother. 20 When Martha heard that Jesus was coming, she went and met him, while Mary stayed at home. 21 Martha said to Jesus, "Lord, if you had been here, my brother would not have died. 22 But even now I know that God will give you whatever you ask of him."

23 Jesus said to her, "Your brother will rise again."

24 Martha said to him, "I know that he will rise again in the resurrection on the last day."

25 Jesus said to her, "I am the resurrection and the life. Those who believe in me, even though they die, will live, 26 and everyone who lives and believes in me will never die. Do you believe this?"

27 She said to him, "Yes, Lord, I believe that you are the Messiah, the Son of God, the one coming into the world."

28 When she had said this, she went back and called her sister Mary, and told her privately, "The Teacher is here and is calling for you." 29 And when she heard it, she got up quickly and went to him. 30 Now Jesus had not yet come to the village, but was still at the place where Martha had met him. . . . 32 When Mary came where Jesus was and saw him, she knelt at his feet and said to him, "Lord, if you had been here, my brother would not have died."

33 When Jesus saw her weeping, and the Jews who came with her also weeping, he was greatly disturbed in spirit and deeply moved. 34 He said, "Where have you laid him?" They said to him, "Lord, come and see." 35 Jesus began to weep. 36 So the Jews said, "See how he loved him!" 37 But some of them said, "Could not he who opened the eyes of the blind man have kept this man from dying?"

38 Then Jesus, again greatly disturbed, came to the tomb. It was a cave, and a stone was lying against it. 39 Jesus said, "Take away the stone."

Martha, the sister of the dead man, said to him, "Lord, already there is a stench because he has been dead four days."

40 Jesus said to her, "Did I not tell you that if you believed, you would see the glory of God?" 41 So they took away the stone. And Jesus looked upward and said, "Father, I thank you for having heard me. 42 I knew that you always hear me, but I have said this for the sake of the crowd standing here, so that they may believe that you sent me." 43 When he had said this, he cried with a loud voice, "Lazarus, come out!" 44 The dead man came out, his hands and feet bound with strips of cloth, and his face wrapped in a cloth. Jesus said to them, "Unbind him, and let him go."

45 Many of the Jews therefore, who had come with Mary and had seen what Jesus did, believed in him.

Another Dinner with Friends

John 12:1 Six days before the Passover Jesus came to Bethany, the home of Lazarus, whom he had raised from the dead. 2 There they gave a dinner for him. Martha served, and Lazarus was one of those at the table with him. 3 Mary took a pound of costly perfume made of pure nard, anointed Jesus' feet, and wiped them with her hair. The house was filled with the fragrance of the perfume.

4 But Judas Iscariot, one of his disciples . . . , said, 5 "Why was this perfume not sold for three hundred denarii and the money given to the poor?" . . . 7 Jesus said, "Leave her alone. She bought it so that she might keep it for the day of my burial. 8 You always have the poor with you, but you do not always have me."

First Impression

5 minutes
Briefly mention a question you have about the reading or one thing in it that surprised, impressed, delighted, or challenged you. No discussion! Just listen to one another's reactions.

Exploring the Theme

If participants have not read this section already, read it aloud.
Otherwise go on to "Questions for Reflection and Discussion."

Luke 10:38–42. Just because Luke does not mention Jesus'
male disciples at this dinner doesn't mean they're not there.
Martha probably has a whole room full of guests. No wonder she is
"distracted" with coming and going between her dining room and
the oven in the corner of her courtyard. Mary should be helping
her, but she cannot pull herself away from Jesus. Letting Martha
carry on alone, Mary sits down and listens. When Martha protests,
Jesus defends Mary's choice. He refuses to allow her to be dislodged
from the role of disciple that she has chosen. He would probably be
happy if Martha, too, would sit down and listen to him. Who cares
if dinner is late? He is more interested in talking about God than
hurrying on to the next meal (see John 4:31–38).

Martha speaks rudely to Jesus (10:40). Surprisingly often,
people are discourteously direct with him. His disciples make bold
and selfish demands (Mark 10:35–37), chide him for failing to
fulfill their expectations (Mark 1:37), dismiss his statements as
nonsensical (Mark 5:31; 6:37), shout at him (Mark 4:38), and
forbid him to carry out his plans (Matthew 16:21–23). It seems
that, for all his gravity and seriousness, Jesus was an approach-
able person, the kind of person to whom people felt comfortable
speaking their mind. These incidents also suggest that many of the
people Jesus chose as friends were pushy, aggressive types. Jesus
seems to have enjoyed strong personalities.

John 11:1–45. Mary and Martha's message to Jesus
about Lazarus states a fact but implies a request: Come right
away! But Jesus does not assent to their request (11:3–6). Again
we are reminded that he alone knows his mission and its timing
(Luke 2:41–51; John 2:1–11; 7:1–10). Jesus refuses to veer an
inch from the path God has marked out for him. On the other hand,
we have seen that Jesus constantly makes himself available to
people who barge in on him or happen to run into him. How he
manages to stay on his assigned course while welcoming the
unexpected is something of a mystery.

Jesus says that Lazarus's illness "is for God's glory"
(11:4). He does not primarily mean that the outcome of his illness

will cause people to praise God. Rather the outcome will reveal God's glory to people; it will show God's life-giving presence in his Son (compare John 2:11). Faced with the apparent illogic of Jesus' decision *not* to go to Martha, Mary, and Lazarus *though* he loved them (11:6), the disciples no doubt continue to find Jesus difficult to understand.

Verse 15 is the only point in John's Gospel where Jesus expresses joy (in the Greek he says literally, "I rejoice"). He is not happy about Lazarus's death. But he is glad for the opportunity to restore Lazarus's life, because this will finally lead his disciples to have faith in him. His disciples' faith in him has been Jesus' goal from the beginning of his public life. Yet even now, at the end of his ministry, they do not fully believe in him.

Jesus delays two days (11:6). When he arrives in Bethany, Lazarus has been dead four days (11:17). Thus, even if Jesus had left for Bethany as soon as he got the sisters' message, he could not have arrived before Lazarus died. Since Jesus' knowledge embraces the whole situation (11:4, 11–14), he must have known when he received the message that he could not arrive in time to save Lazarus from dying. Thus he did not delay in order to give time for Lazarus to die. Whatever the reason was for Jesus' delay—John does not explain it—his delay did not cause Lazarus additional pain.

Obviously, Martha and Mary know when they sent their message to Jesus and when their brother died. Presumably they also know how long it would take Jesus to travel to Bethany. So they, too, know that he could not have arrived before their brother's death. Thus their plaintive statement—"Lord, if you had been here, my brother would not have died" (11:21, 32)—is not a reproach for not coming sooner. It is a statement of continuing faith: "Even in this world of sickness and death, we believe that you are the savior." This is a great statement of faith: the sisters believe that Jesus can sustain life in the face of everything that endangers it. But they do not yet believe that Jesus can reverse death and restore life. They believe that God will raise the dead on the last day (11:24). But they do not believe that Jesus possesses this death-conquering power here and now (11:25–27), as we can see from Martha's protest at Jesus' command to open Lazarus's tomb. They regard him as a powerful intermediary with God (11:22). They have not grasped that he and the Father are one (John 10:30).

Jesus' tears in this scene are usually taken as a sign of his grief at death's power over his friend Lazarus—a grief so intense that it rips him apart even though he knows he is about to bring Lazarus back to life. But the very fact that the crowd interprets Jesus' weeping as an expression of love for Lazarus (11:33–35) alerts us to the possibility that there is more to it, since in John's Gospel the crowds usually take a somewhat inaccurate view of Jesus. In fact, other sorrows also feed into the torrent of Jesus' grief. He bears the frustration of knowing that he is the Resurrection, that he alone offers the solution to death, yet not even those who are closest to him have come to believe this. The Greek word translated "disturbed" (11:33) strikes a tone of indignation; it suggests angry disapproval (elsewhere it is translated "sternly ordered," "sternly warning," and "scolded"—Matthew 9:30; Mark 1:43; 14:5). New Testament scholar Francis J. Moloney, S.D.B., writes: "As Jesus' public ministry draws to a close, he is frustrated and angrily disappointed . . . and this is manifested in a deep, shuddering internal emotion. . . . Will no one come to belief?" Another commentator remarks that the bystanders did not perceive that Jesus' tears were more over them than over Lazarus (compare Luke 19:41–44).

At Lazarus's tomb (11:38) Jesus is again deeply disturbed. Perhaps now dread is added to sorrow and anger. By coming to the aid of Lazarus, Jesus has taken a step toward his own death. Weeping by Lazarus's tomb in sorrow for death as the end of all human life, Jesus weeps as one of us, facing his own end. More than once in the coming days, he will experience an almost violent revulsion as his death approaches (John 12:27; 13:21).

But now, rising above all sorrow, Jesus' voice rings out, powerful and clear. "Lazarus, come out!" he cries. And Lazarus comes out.

The raising of Lazarus is both the climax of Jesus' ministry and the trigger for the events that will result in his death. While some of the crowd celebrate Lazarus's return to life (11:45), others go off and report it to the temple council, spurring the council to decide to have Jesus put to death (11:46–53). Jesus has returned to Jerusalem to bring his friend back to life, knowing that he will pay with his own life for this act of kindness.

John 12:1–8. Not long afterward, Jesus is the guest of honor at the home of Martha, Mary, and Lazarus. Mary's gesture of honor with perfumed oil is extravagant, but who can blame her? No one could object but a person in whose heart love for money and bitterness have taken root (12:4–6). Once again, Jesus defends Mary against criticism. She may not fully understand who Jesus is—or the significance of her own action (12:7)—but her love for Jesus is genuine. Her heart is leading her in the right direction.

Reclining next to Jesus as Mary pours out her oil is her brother Lazarus. Having raised Lazarus from the dead, Jesus shares a meal with him, while he himself is anointed for burial. Now that he has called Lazarus out of his tomb, Jesus prepares to enter his own. Jesus has traded places with his friend.

Reflection. Twice in these readings (Luke 10:41–42; John 12:7–8) Jesus rebuffs those who appeal to him to correct an apparent injustice by Mary. How often throughout our readings Jesus has rejected criticisms or complaints made against another person. The religious people who complain about the toll collectors, Simon who mentally criticizes the woman who intrudes on his banquet, the accusers of the woman who was committing adultery, the man who seeks help against his brother in an inheritance matter, the disciples who want to strike down the inhospitable Samaritans, Martha and Judas who complain about Mary's devotion to Jesus—Jesus rejects every complaint and accusation. Often he turns the complaint or criticism around and spurs the one who brought it to look into his or her own heart.

Questions for Reflection and Discussion

45 minutes
Choose questions according to your interest and time.

1 Which of the two sisters do you think was the older? Why?

2 In John 11:1–45, how many times does Jesus speak about people coming to believe in him? How important to him does this seem to be?

3 Compare John 11:39 with John 2:5 (Week 1). How does Martha's faith in Jesus compare with that of his mother?

4 What opportunity is Jesus giving you to sit and listen to him? How can you take advantage of it?

5 When has your criticism of someone or complaint against them spurred you to examine yourself and your own values more carefully?

6 For personal reflection: Mary seems irresponsible in the way she devotes her attention to Jesus, and extravagant in the way that she expresses her love for him. Have you ever been like Mary? What does Jesus' approval of Mary suggest about how he invites you to relate to him?

7 **Focus question:** What is the essence of friendship? In these readings, what aspects of friendship can be seen between Jesus and Martha, Mary, and Lazarus? What clues does Jesus' behavior offer for how you might cultivate friendship with others?

Prayer to Close

10 minutes
Use this approach—or create your own!

◆ Begin with an Our Father. Pray this litany, with the response, "Save us, O Son of God, who are risen from the dead. Alleluia, alleluia, alleluia." Add further petitions if you like. End with a Hail Mary and Glory Be.

In our busyness and distractions—

Save us, O Son of God, who are risen from the dead. Alleluia, alleluia, alleluia.

In our difficulty trusting you fully—

Save us, O Son of God, who are risen from the dead. Alleluia, alleluia, alleluia.

In our grief at the loss of those we have loved—

Save us, O Son of God, who are risen from the dead. Alleluia, alleluia, alleluia.

In all our work, our sorrows, our joys, our friendships, our hopes—

Save us, O Son of God, who are risen from the dead. Alleluia, alleluia, alleluia.

A Living Tradition

Bethany Decisions

(Luke 10:38–42)

This section is a supplement for individual reading.

As Jesus taught the gathered brothers
and Martha boiled and baked their dinner,
Mary eavesdropped in the anteroom
between the great hall and the kitchen.
Her dying mother's warning words
clanged clearly in her memory—
"Obey your sister. She has learned
the ways and duties of a woman."

She'd learned her sister's lessons well
and knew a woman's place was *not*
to sit and listen and be taught.
But when she heard the voice of Jesus
call to her above the din
of Martha's boiling pots and pans,
she made her choice decisively—
took off her apron and traditions,
and walked in.

   —Irene Zimmerman, O.S.F.

A Closer Look at Jesus' Family

Our readings in Week 1 raise some questions about Jesus' family. Mary seems to be keenly attuned to Jesus at Cana (in John's Gospel). But later in his public life (in Mark's Gospel) she appears with Jesus' brothers when they come to seize him because they have heard he has gone out of his mind. How could Mary take part in such an action? And, since the Church regards Mary as having remained a virgin throughout her life, who *were* these brothers of Jesus? Let's begin with the first question.

The presence of different views of Mary in the Gospels stems from two factors. The Gospel authors had different sources of information—different oral traditions and different written sources—when they sat down to write their accounts of Jesus. And the Gospel authors emphasized different aspects of Jesus' life and teaching in order to serve the particular groups of Christians for whom they were writing. As a result, we have four distinct portraits of Jesus. Each is a true portrait, but the portraits are different from each other, somewhat the way the portraits of one person by four painters might be different.

Each of the Gospel portraits of Jesus includes a distinctive view of his mother. Of the Gospel writers, Mark is the least concerned with Mary. In fact, he hardly includes her. The episode we read in Week 1 (Mark 3:19–35) is the only one in Mark's Gospel in which Mary plays a part (Mark mentions her once more in 6:3). Why did she go along with the men in the family when they came to take charge of Jesus? What did she think? Mark does not tell us. He has written a sparse narrative and has left many questions—about Jesus as well as Mary—unanswered. Only in the other three Gospels, especially Luke and John, do we find a portrait, or at least a sketch, of Jesus' mother.

John shows Mary with Jesus at the beginning and the end of his public life, an arrangement that suggests she was somehow connected with his whole mission. Mary is with Jesus at Cana, when he first reveals himself through a miracle, and at Calvary, where he perfectly reveals his love for his Father by giving his life for us. At both points, Mary is mysteriously aligned with Jesus' purposes.

At Cana, Mary spurs Jesus to perform his first miracle. She demonstrates faith in him, even though she does not understand him. Throughout his ministry, Jesus tries to move people toward complete faith in him, but no one explicitly attains this goal until after his death and resurrection, when Thomas acknowledges him as "My Lord and my God!" (John 20:28). In John's portrayal of Mary at Cana, however, he seems to suggest that Mary had attained this faith in Jesus even before he began his public life.

At Calvary, Jesus places his mother in the care of a male disciple who is especially deep in his affection (John 19:26–27). Jesus seems not only to give his mother into the disciple's care but also to give the disciple into his mother's care. Given the multiple levels of meaning throughout John's Gospel, Jesus evidently means something more than that these two beloved people should care for each other after his death. Jesus is giving his mother not only to this one disciple but to all his disciples, present and future.

Luke is equally interested in Mary. He shows an angel announcing to her that she will be the mother of the Messiah and recounts her willingness to play her part in God's plan (Luke 1:26–38). Luke shows Mary struggling to understand her son, thinking carefully about all that is revealed to her (Luke 2:19, 51). Thus Luke presents Mary as the model disciple: she believes God's word, obeys God, and ponders the mystery of God's love in his Son. In Luke's account in Acts, Mary makes her final appearance among Jesus' disciples (Acts 1:14). The implication is that her relationship with her son's followers will continue on into the future.

John and Luke probably wrote some years after Mark. If so, their Gospels are evidence that the early Christians were increasingly turning their attention to Mary, preserving traditions about her, and reflecting on her significance for the community of Jesus' followers. Later generations of Christians continued this line of reflection. As they pondered and prayed, their love for Mary deepened, and a larger, clearer picture of her emerged. Confidence grew that she continues to participate in the life of the Church as a powerful intercessor with God because of her intimate union with her son. And the belief emerged that Mary had remained a virgin throughout her life as an expression of her total devotion to God. The early Christians reached this conviction as they reflected on the picture of Mary in the Gospels and pondered traditions about her that were not written down.

Since Mary's permanent virginity is not stated explicitly in the New Testament but only suggested, the question of the authenticity of this belief arises. The fundamental answer is that the truth of the belief is assured by its affirmation by the Church.

To explain how this can be requires a little digression to consider the Lord's continuing presence with the Church. Jesus promised that he would remain with the Church, always guiding the community of his followers by his Spirit (Matthew 28:18–20; John 14:15–21, 25–28; 15:26–16:15). He protects the community from straying from the truth about him and leads it into growing understanding. After Jesus' death and resurrection, the Holy Spirit came to his followers to amplify and deepen their faith in him. From the earliest days of the Christian community until today, the Lord has never stopped providing his guidance.

Consequently, as the Church prays, explores, and lives its faith in Christ, it comes to a deeper grasp of all that God has revealed in his Son. The bishops who gathered at the Second Vatican Council (1962–65) said: "The Tradition that comes from the apostles makes progress in the Church, with the help of the Holy Spirit. There is a growth in insight into the realities and words that are being passed on" (*Dogmatic Constitution on Divine Revelation,* section 8). The bishops said this process continues as believers study and pray about their faith in Christ and as the bishops, who are successors of the apostles, preach and teach. "Thus, as the centuries go by, the Church is always advancing toward the plenitude of divine truth" (*Dogmatic Constitution on Divine Revelation,* section 8). Because all the members of the Church have received the Holy Spirit, the bishops declared, "The whole body of the faithful . . . cannot err in matters of belief," so long as the whole body remains united with the bishops and their teaching (*Dogmatic Constitution on the Church,* section 12).

The Church's belief that Mary remained a virgin throughout her life is a classic example of this process by which there is "growth in insight into the realities and words that are being passed on." The New Testament clearly teaches that Mary bore Jesus as a virgin (Matthew 1:18; Luke 1:34–35). While her perpetual virginity after Jesus' birth is not explicitly stated in the New Testament, the early tradition of the Church testifies to the presence of this belief, although we have no written historical sources to confirm it. The conviction that Mary remained a virgin after the birth of Jesus was carried in a hidden tradition, like an underground stream that gradually came to the surface and flowed out into the open. By the early fifth century, the belief in Mary's perpetual virginity was accepted throughout the entire Church.

Given Jesus' ongoing guidance of the Church by his Spirit, it is enough for later maturing doctrines, such as Mary's perpetual virginity, to be in continuity with Scripture. They do not need to be supported explicitly in the Bible. Certainly, however, they cannot be in contradiction to Scripture. Yet some people argue that the belief in Mary's permanent virginity *does* conflict with the New Testament. Specifically, they say, the belief in Mary's perpetual virginity is contradicted by the presence of brothers and sisters of Jesus in the New Testament.

At one point during his public life, Jesus visits his hometown of Nazareth. The townspeople say, "Is not this the carpenter's son? Is not his mother called Mary? And are not his brothers James and Joseph and Simon and Judas? And are not all his sisters with us?" (Matthew 13:55–56; compare Mark 6:3). Paul writes that when he visited the Christians in Jerusalem, he "did not see any other apostle except James the Lord's brother" (Galatians 1:19; compare Acts 12:17; 15:13; 21:18; 1 Corinthians 15:7; Galatians 2:9, 12). In one of our readings in Week 1, we witnessed a conversation between Jesus and his "brothers" (John 7:1–10). From our English versions of the New Testament, the conclusion might seem obvious: Jesus had brothers and sisters; these were children of Mary; therefore, Mary did not remain a virgin through her whole life. But the matter is not so simple.

The New Testament was not written in English but in Greek. And behind the Greek of the New Testament lies the Aramaic spoken by Jesus, his family, and the disciples. (Aramaic was a first cousin of Hebrew.) In Aramaic, the words translated into English as *brother* and *sister* have a wide range of meanings. Aramaic lacked words for stepbrother or cousin, so the word for brother served for those relationships, too. Thus, in Aramaic-speaking Galilee, to call someone a "brother" or "sister" did not strictly define the relationship. A "brother" or "sister" might be a sibling or a more distant relative. Likewise, in the Hebrew of the Old Testament, the term *brother* might be applied to someone who was in fact a nephew (Genesis 24:48; 29:12), a cousin (1 Chronicles 23:22), or simply a kinsman (Jeremiah 12:6). Greek had more specific terms for these relationships (Paul uses the Greek word for "cousin" in Colossians 4:10). But sometimes the New Testament writers followed the Hebrew and Aramaic usage and used the Greek word for "brother" for someone who was not a full sibling. For example, the Gospel writers mention a Philip as the "brother" of Herod Antipas, even though the two men were half brothers, sons of different mothers (Matthew 14:3; Mark 6:17). Thus the words *brother* and *sister* in the New Testament do not by themselves tell us the precise relationship that existed between these family members and Jesus.

Is there other information that might help us determine the relationship between Jesus and his brothers and sisters? Within the Gospels, there is at least one strand of evidence. Two of the men called brothers of Jesus in Matthew's and Mark's Gospels (Matthew 13:55; Mark 6:3) seem to be mentioned later as sons of a woman other than Jesus' mother (Matthew 27:56; Mark 15:40). How the mother of these two men was related to Jesus is not explained, thus the men's relationship to Jesus cannot be clarified with certainty. Perhaps they were cousins. In any case, they seem not to have been Jesus' siblings.

After the Gospels were written, Christians came to two different views of the relationship between Jesus and his "brothers" and "sisters," probably on the basis of different oral traditions. Jerome, a Latin-speaking biblical scholar who lived in Bethlehem in the late fourth century, explained that the brothers and sisters of Jesus were his cousins. At about the same time, Epiphanius, a Greek-speaking bishop on the island of Cyprus who had grown up in Palestine, explained that they were children of Joseph by a previous marriage.

St. Jerome's explanation became accepted throughout the Latin-speaking Church, that is, the Church that spread throughout western Europe. Jerome's view implied that Joseph remained a virgin throughout his life. Thus, as devotion to St. Joseph developed in western Europe, he came to be regarded as a model for virgins. That is why he is often shown holding a lily, a symbol of virginity.

Epiphanius's view became accepted by Greek-speaking Christians. As the Greek-speaking, or Byzantine, sector of the Church spread in the Middle East and eastern Europe, Christians there accepted the view of Joseph as a widower. This is the view held today not only by Eastern Orthodox Christians but also by Byzantine Catholics in communion with the Pope. In the Byzantine tradition of icons, Joseph the widower came to be depicted as an old man (although obviously widowers can be young).

Within the Catholic Church, the Latin and the Greek traditions on this matter have equal standing. There is no definitive Church teaching confirming or denying either view.

During Jesus' lifetime, his brothers did not believe in him. But after his death and resurrection, some of them came to a different view. After Jesus appeared to James, James became one of his key followers (see Acts 12:17; 15:13; 21:18; 1 Corinthians 15:7; Galatians 1:19; 2:9, 12). For more than twenty years, from about AD 40, James led the church in Jerusalem. He is considered to be the author of the New Testament writing called the letter of James. The high priest Ananus had him stoned to death in the sixties.

Luke also mentions that some of the "brothers" of Jesus belonged to the Christian community in Jerusalem even before Pentecost (Acts 1:14). Presumably, Luke meant his "sisters," too.

Suggestions for Bible Discussion Groups

L ike a camping trip, a Bible discussion group works best if you agree on where you're going and how you intend to get there. Many groups use their first meeting to talk over such questions. Here is a checklist of issues, with bits of advice from people who have experience in Bible discussions. (A planning discussion will go more smoothly if the leaders have thought through the following issues beforehand.)

Agree on your purpose. Are you getting together to gain wisdom and direction for your lives? to finally get acquainted with the Bible? to support one another in following Christ? to encourage those who are exploring—or reexploring—the Church? for other reasons?

Agree on attitudes. For example: "We're all beginners here." "We're here to help one another understand and respond to God's word." "We're not here to offer counseling or direction to one another." "We want to read Scripture prayerfully." What do *you* wish to emphasize? Make it explicit!

Agree on ground rules. Barbara J. Fleischer, in her useful book *Facilitating for Growth,* recommends that a group clearly state its approach to the following:

- ◆ *Preparation.* Do we agree to read the material and prepare answers to the questions before each meeting?
- ◆ *Attendance.* What kind of priority will we give to our meetings?
- ◆ *Self-revelation.* Are we willing to help the others in the group gradually get to know us—our weaknesses as well as our strengths, our needs as well as our gifts?
- ◆ *Listening.* Will we commit ourselves to listen to one another?
- ◆ *Confidentiality.* Will we keep everything that is shared *with* the group *in* the group?
- ◆ *Discretion.* Will we refrain from sharing about the faults and sins of people who are not in the group?
- ◆ *Encouragement and support.* Will we give as well as receive?
- ◆ *Participation.* Will we give each person the time and opportunity to make a contribution?

You could probably take a pen and draw a circle around *listening* and *confidentiality*. Those two points are especially important.

The following items could be added to Fleischer's list:

◆ *Relationship with parish.* Is our group part of the adult faith-formation program? independent but operating with the express approval of the pastor? not a parish-based group?

◆ *New members.* Will we let new members join us once we have begun the six weeks of discussions?

Agree on housekeeping.

◆ *When will we meet?*

◆ *How often will we meet?* Meeting weekly or every other week is best if you can manage it. William Riley remarks, "Meetings once a month are too distant from each other for the threads of the last session not to be lost" *(The Bible Study Group: An Owner's Manual).*

◆ *How long will each meeting run?*

◆ *Where will we meet?*

◆ *Is any setup needed?* Christine Dodd writes that "the problem with meeting in a place like a church hall is that it can be very soul-destroying" given the cold, impersonal feel of many church facilities. If you have to meet in a church facility, Dodd recommends doing something to make the area homey *(Making Scripture Work).*

◆ *Who will host the meetings?* Leaders and hosts are not necessarily the same people.

◆ *Will we have refreshments?* Who will provide them? Don Cousins and Judson Poling make this recommendation: "Serve refreshments if you like, but save snacks and other foods for the end of the meeting to minimize distraction" *(Leader's Guide 1).*

◆ *What about child care?* Most experienced leaders of Bible discussion groups discourage bringing infants or other children to adult Bible discussions.

Agree on leadership. You need someone to facilitate—to keep the discussion on track, to see that everyone has a chance to speak, to help the group stay on schedule. Rena Duff, editor of the newsletter *Sharing God's Word Today,* recommends having two or three people take turns leading the discussions.

It's okay if the leader is not an expert on the Bible. You have this Six Weeks book as a guide, and if questions come up that no one can answer, you can delegate a participant to do a little research between meetings. Perhaps someone on the pastoral staff of your parish could offer advice. Or help may be available from your diocesan catechetical office or a local Catholic college or seminary.

It's important for the leader to set an example of listening, to draw out the quieter members (and occasionally restrain the more vocal ones), to move the group on when it gets stuck, to get the group back on track when the discussion moves away from the topic, and to restate and summarize what the group is learning. Sometimes the leader needs to remind the members of their agreements. An effective group leader is enthusiastic about the topic and the discussions and sets an example of learning from others and of using resources for growing in understanding.

As a discussion group matures, other members of the group will increasingly share in doing all these things on their own initiative.

Bible discussion is an opportunity to experience the fulfillment of Jesus' promise "Where two or three are gathered in my name, I am there among them" (Matthew 18:20). Put your discussion group in Jesus' hands. Pray for the guidance of the Spirit. And have a great time exploring God's word together!

Suggestions for Individuals

Y ou can use this booklet just as well for individual study as for group discussion. While discussing the Bible with other people can be a rich experience, there are advantages to reading on your own. For example:

◆ You can focus on the points that interest you most.

◆ You can go at your own pace.

◆ You can be completely relaxed and unashamedly honest in your answers to all the questions, since you don't have to share them with anyone!

My suggestions for using this book on your own are these:

◆ Don't skip "Questions to Begin" or "First Impression."

◆ Take your time on "Questions for Reflection and Discussion." While a group will probably not have enough time to work on all the questions, you can allow yourself the time to consider all of them If you are using the book by yourself.

◆ After reading "Exploring the Theme," go back and reread the Scripture text before answering the "Questions for Reflection and Discussion."

◆ Take the time to look up all the parenthetical Scripture references.

◆ Read additional sections of Scripture related to the excerpts in this book. For example, read the portions of Scripture that come before and after the sections that form the readings in this Six Weeks book. You will understand the readings better by viewing them in context in the Bible.

◆ Since you control the pace, give yourself plenty of opportunities to reflect on the meaning of the Scripture passages for you. Let your reading be an opportunity for these words to become God's words to you.

Bibles

The following editions of the Bible contain the full set of biblical books recognized by the Catholic Church, along with a great deal of useful explanatory material:

◆ The Catholic Study Bible (Oxford University Press), which uses the text of the New American Bible

◆ The Catholic Bible: Personal Study Edition (Oxford University Press), which also uses the text of the New American Bible

◆ The New Jerusalem Bible, the regular (not the reader's) edition (Doubleday)

Books, Web Sites, and Other Resources

◆ For more information on the Catholic Evidence Guild (p. 35), see www.catholicevidence.org.

◆ For more information on Azim Khamisa and the Tariq Khamisa Foundation (p. 71), see www.tkf.org.

How has Scripture had an impact on your life? Was this booklet helpful to you in your study of the Bible? Please send comments, suggestions, and personal experiences to Kevin Perrotta, General Editor, Trade Editorial Department, Loyola Press, 3441 N. Ashland Ave., Chicago, IL 60657.